The ESSENTIALS® of
REGISTERED TRADEMARK

C

Programming Language

D0063341

Ernest C. Ackermann, Ph.D.

Chairperson of Computer Science Department
Mary Washington College, Fredericksburg, VA

Research and Education Association
61 Ethel Road West
Piscataway, New Jersey 08854

THE ESSENTIALS ®
OF C PROGRAMMING

Printed in the United States of America

Library of Congress Catalog Card Number 89-62092

International Standard Book Number 0-87891-696-2

REVISED PRINTING, 1993

WHAT "THE ESSENTIALS" WILL DO FOR YOU

This book is a review and study guide. It is comprehensive and it is concise.

It helps in preparing for exams, in doing homework, and remains a handy reference source at all times.

It condenses the vast amount of detail characteristic of the subject matter and summarizes the **essentials** of the field.

It will thus save hours of study and preparation time.

The book provides quick access to the important facts, principles, and concepts in the field.

Materials needed for exams can be reviewed in summary form – eliminating the need to read and re-read many pages of textbook and class notes. The summaries will even tend to bring detail to mind that had been previously read or noted.

This "ESSENTIALS" book has been prepared by an expert in the field, and has been carefully reviewed to assure accuracy and maximum usefulness.

Dr. Max Fogiel
Program Director

CONTENTS

CHAPTER 1

FUNDAMENTAL NOTIONS

C was originally designed, in the 1970's, for the UNIX operating system by Dennis Ritchie at Bell Laboratories. In 1978 the book *The C Programming Language*, by Brian Kernighan and Dennis Ritchie, was published. That book contained a definition of C which has been used as a basis for many of the current versions of C. In 1983 the American National Standards Institute (ANSI) established a committee to define a standard for C. The ANSI standard for C will be finally approved in late 1989 or 1990. There are many versions of C and all major versions adhere to the specifications in the Kernighan & Ritchie (K&R) book or they conform to the standard.

The ANSI standard formalizes many of the topics or notions introduced in K&R. It includes a standard library and requires the declaration of functions so that the compiler may check the number, type, and order of arguments to functions. We will use the notation of the ANSI standard throughout this text so that a function will be declared specifying the types of its parameters. Another name for this type of declaration is a **prototype**. The examples in this book can be used with versions of C which don't allow prototypes by changing each declaration of the form

```
funname( type1, type2, type3)
```
to

1

funname( )

In the chapter that deals with functions we will explicitly show the differences between K&R versions and the ANSI standard.

1.1   A C SOURCE PROGRAM

A program written in C is a collection of functions and variables. The functions contain statements and the variables hold the results of computations. Every C program must contain one function named **main**. All variables must be declared, either within a function or outside of any function.

The sample program below contains two functions, **main** and **average**. **main** begins on line 6 and ends on line 21. It is declared as **main(void)** which indicates it has no formal parameters. All the local variables and statements of **main()** are between the { on line 7 and the matching } on line 22. The specification of the function **average** begins on line 26 and ends on line 34. **average** has two parameters, **a** and **n**. **a** represents an array of objects of type float and **n** represents an object of type integer. **average** also has some local variables and statements associated with it. These are on lines 28 through 30.

```
1   /*
2   **example c program
3   */
4   #include "stdio.h"
5   #define MAX 1000
6   main(void)
7   {
8      int num_in,k,j;
9      float in_val,sizes[MAX];
10     float average(float a[ ],n);
11
12     num_in = 0;
13     printf("Please enter a value. A negative value stops entry ==> ");
14     scanf("%f",&in_val);
15     while( in_val >= 0 && num_in < MAX-1){
```

2

```
16    sizes[num_in++] = in_val;
17    printf ("Please enter a value. A negative value stops entry ==> ");
18    scanf("%f",&in_val);
19    }
20    printf(" Average of %d items input = %6.3f\n",num_in,
21                                     average (sizes, num_in) );
22  }
23  /*function average
24  **   computes average value of array a with n items
25  */
26  float average(float a[ ],int n)
27  {
28    float s;
29    int i;
30    s = 0;
31    for (i = 0; i < n; i++)
32      s = s + a[i];
33    return(s/n);
34  }
```

A program in C usually contains comments and directives to a preprocessor. Lines 1 – 3 and 23 – 25 are comments. A preprocessor performs macro substitution, conditional compilation, and file inclusion. The lines beginning with # are preprocessor directives. In this program we request that the file stdio.h be included with the program before it is translated and define the symbol MAX to be 100.

1.2   TOKENS, COMMENTS, AND WHITESPACE

A source program in C is translated into executable code. In the early stages of that translation the compiler will group the characters of the program into lexical units called **tokens**. The five types of tokens are identifiers, keywords, operators, separators, and constants. Consider the statement:

    box_top =y[2   ]+1.423; /*move top of box*/

The tokens in that statement are the identifiers **box_top** and **y**,

3

the operators = and +, the separators [,], and ;, and the constants **2** and **1.423**. The other characters in that statement are either comments or whitespace.

The two characters /* start a comment and the two characters */ end a comment. Comments may occur anywhere except that /* and */ are not interpreted as comment delimeters when they occur within string literals. For example,

x = "this comment marker /* is ignored"; /* here's the comment*/

Comments may not be nested so that the following consists of one comment followed by the characters **outer** */.

/* outer /*inner comment*/ outer /*

Spaces, horizontal and vertical tabs, newlines, formfeeds, and comments are known as "whitespace". Whitespace is ignored by the translator except as it is necessary to separate some identifiers, keywords, or operators. For example, whitespace is necessary to separate the keywords and identifer name on the following line:

static int count;

However, any whitespace between count and ; (the semicolon) is ignored. Also, the following two lines have the same meaning:

x = z + y;
x=z+y;

So whitespace is ignored unless it is necessary to specify the meaning of a string of characters. Naturally, it's a good practice to use it to improve the readability of a program.

1.3 IDENTIFIERS

Identifiers are used to name variables, functions, types, and labels. An identifier is a sequence of letters (upper or lower case), the underscore character '_' and/or digits. The first character in the sequence must be a letter. The translator differentiates upper from lower case letters. The first 31 characters of local identifiers, those used within a single function, are significant. Only the first six characters may be significant for identifiers that are shared through the use of external linkage. This is implementation dependent. The following are all valid and different identifiers: **Abc23, abc23, ab_c23, aBc23, and ABC23**. Variables and functions are generally written with only lowercase letters. Constants and macro names are generally written using uppercase letters as in the following program fragment which initializes the elements of the array **clown_aray** to the value stored in **bobo**:

```
#define MAX 100
main(void)
{        int i, bobo, clown_aray[MAX];
•
∞

         for ( i = 0; i < MAX; i++ )
            clown_aray[i] = bobo;
•
•
```

1.4   KEYWORDS

Some names are reserved for use as keywords and may not be used for any other purpose. The keywords are:

auto	double	int	struct
break	else	long	switch
case	enum	register	typedef
char	extern	return	union
const	float	short	unsigned
continue	for	signed	void
default	goto	sizeof	volatile
do	if	static	while

It's more instructive to group the keywords into categories

that fit their function or purpose. A good deal of the remainder of this text deals with the use and meaning of these keywords.

labels:	case, default
operator:	sizeof
program control:	break, case, continue, default, do, else, for, goto, if, return, switch, while
storage class:	auto, extern, register, static, typedef
type specifiers:	char, double, enum, float, int, long, short, signed, struct, union, unsigned, void
type qualifiers:	const, volatile

1.5 OPERATORS AND SEPARATORS

C has a particularly large set of operators. They are:

Operator	Name	Operator	Name
!	logical NOT	~	bitwise complement
−	arithmetic	*	indirection
&	address of	+	unary plus
+	addition	−	subtraction
*	multiplication	/	division
%	remainder	<<	left shift
>>	right shift	<	less than
<=	less than or equal	>	greater than
>=	greater than or equal	==	equal
!=	not equal	&	bitwise AND
		bitwise inclusive OR	^	bitwise exclusive OR
&&	logical AND	||	logical OR
,	sequential evaluation	?:	conditional
++	increment	−−	decrement
=	simple assignment	+=	addition assignment
−=	subtraction assign- ment	*=	multiplication assign- ment
/=	division assignment	%=	remainder assign- ment
>>=	right shift assignment		

6

&=	bitwise AND assignment	<<=	left shift assignment
^=	bitwise exclusive OR assignment	| =	bitwise inclusive OR assignment

The separators are ( ) [ ] { } , ; :

1.6 CONSTANTS

Here we discuss tokens which are referred to in some languages as **literals**. Their values are specified explicitly and never change.

1.6.1 INTEGER CONSTANTS

Integer constants may be expressed in octal, decimal, or hexadecimal notation. A decimal integer consists of a sequence of digits the first of which is not zero. An octal representation of an integer consists of a sequence of digits in the range 0-7, and the first digit must be 0. A hexadecimal representation of an integer consists of the digit 0, followed by either **x** or **X**, and then a sequence of hexadecimal digits (0 – 9, A – F, a – f). For example, the integer four hundred twenty-seven is represented as **427 in decimal, 0653 in octal**, and **oX1ab in hexadecimal**.

1.6.2 FLOATING POINT CONSTANTS

Floating point constants are always written in decimal (base ten) notation. They contain a decimal point, a signed exponent, or both. For example 0.4, 4.0, 4e–1, 423.3455e+2.

1.6.3 CHARACTER CONSTANTS

A character constant is a sequence of one or more characters enclosed in single quotes. The following are examples of character constants:

'a' '#' '\n'.

The character constant single quote (') cannot be represented by surrounding it with a pair of single quotes. Other characters can't be represented in this way either. The following escape sequences may be used to represent them.

\n	newline	NL	\\	backslash	\
\t	horizontal tab	HT	\?	question mark	?
\v	vertical tab	VT	\'	single quote	'
\b	backspace	BS	\"	double quote	"
\r	carriage return	CR	\ooo	octal number	ooo
\f	formfeed	FF	\xhh	hex number	hh
\a	audible alert	BEL			

It is possible to represent characters by their ASCII code expressed in octal or hexadecimal form. For example, Control-H the backspace character may be represented by '\b', '\010', or '\x08'.

1.6.4   STRING CONSTANTS

A string constant is a sequence of characters between double quotes such as "Hello World!". Strings and characters are not the same. A sequence of characters is just that, but a string is a sequence of characters whose last character marks the end of the string. This character is the character whose value is zero. It may be represented as \000 or NULL. The language system provides this character when string constants are used; it is not provided by the writer of the program. So "Hello World!" is a string constant representing the exclamation. Although the NULL is not visible, it is provided by the language system and marks the end of the string. By contrast, 'Hello World!' is a sequence of characters – not a string.

CHAPTER 2

DATA TYPES AND DATA OBJECTS: SPECIFICATION AND REPRESENTATION

A data object holds a collection of bits. The manner in which those bits are interpreted determines the data value of the object. A data type is a collection of data objects along with the operations defined on those objects. In this chapter we will discuss the specification and representation of data objects available in C. The operations will be dealt with in the next chapter.

A classification of the types available is:

void
arithmetic types: **integral –**   char, int, enum
                                   floating –   float, double
          derived types: arrays, functions, pointers, structures, unions

2.1   THE VOID TYPE

The type void indicates no data, an empty set of data. It is used to specify the type of a function which returns no values. For example:

    void prn2d(int d)

```
{ printf("%d\n",2*d); }
```

prints the value of d multiplied by 2 and a newline character.

2.2 ARITHMETIC TYPES

Objects of arithmetic types can be interpreted as numbers.

2.2.1 INTEGRAL

There is a larger variety of integral types available in C
than in many other languages. This reflects the architecture and
operations found on most computers. One of the design goals
of C was to provide a close correspondence between the language and the underlying machine. Integral types are used to
represent characters, to represent signed and unsigned integers,
to provide for boolean values (0 for FALSE and 1 for TRUE),
and to represent enumerated types as found in many languages
such as Pascal. There is no boolean type per se, but the values
0 and 1 can be used effectively as will be seen in the chapter on
expressions.

The first bit of objects of these types is used to represent
the sign (positive or negative) of the represented value unless
the object is declared **unsigned**. This bit is called the **sign bit**.
If they are declared unsigned then there is one more bit available to represent a value.

2.2.1.1 char OR character

Objects of type char, characters, can be used to store any
member of the executable character set. Initially this included
ASCII and EBCDIC so that one byte was sufficient. The ANSI
standard includes provision for also representing international
character sets. A char object can be declared **signed** or **unsigned**. Both occupy the same amount of space. On machines
that use a byte to represent an object of type char, such an
object may be used to represent integers in the range 0 to 127.
On the same machine an unsigned char may be used to repre-

10

sent an integer in the range 0 to 255.

2.2.1.2 int OR integer

Objects of type integer can be used to store any integer that may be represented on the underlying machine. So the range of values that can be represented is termed **machine dependent**.

There are three sizes of objects of type integer. They are **short int, int,** and **long int.** Furthermore, each may also be **unsigned**.

int — Objects of this type are integers, positive, negative and zero that are representable by the host computer. The range of values available may differ from one implementation to another. For example, on a machine which uses 16 bits to represent integers the values available range from -32768 to 32767 (-2^{15} through $2^{15} - 1$).

unsigned int — Objects of this type are either positive or zero. They have the same representation as int except that the first bit that is used to represent the sign in an object of type int is available for data. So on a machine which uses 16 bits to represent an integer the unsigned int range is from 0 to 65535.

short int — Objects of this type are integers in the range -32768 to 32767. They may differ from those of type int depending on the underlying hardware.

unsigned short int — Objects of this type are either positive integers or zero in the range 0 to 65535.

long int —Objects of this type are integers which are at least in the range -2147483648 to 2147483647. This implies that 32 bits are used to represent a long integer. A wider range may be possible on some machines.

unsigned long int — Objects of this type are either positive integers or zero in the range 0 to at least 4294967295.

11

2.2.1.3 enum OR enumerations

Enumerated types are data types created by the programmer. The operations are the same as those for any integer, but the programmer determines the possible values for objects of that type. Consider:

```
enum color { red, orange, yellow, green, blue, indigo, violet };
```

Here the tag color is the name of the type and its possible values are listed within the braces. These values may be used wherever an integer constant may be used. For example,

```
enum color { red, orange, yellow, green, blue, indigo, violet };
color i;
for (i = red; i <= violet; i++)
```

In this case red is given the value 0 and violet the value 6. Other values may be specified in a program. For example, **enum rooms { lab=204, class=203, printers=5, terminals=5, lounge=109 }** or **enum courses { assembly=301, organization, datastruct }**. In the last example **assembly** has the value 301, **organization** has the value 302, and **datastruct** has the value 303.

2.2.2 FLOATING

Floating point, or real, data objects are used to store numeric values which contain a decimal point. They are available in two sizes, float (single precision) and double (double precision). Examples of floating point constants were given in section 1.6.2. Examples of declarations of floating point objects are

```
double max ( float x, inty) float x_force[10] float x_coord double pi
```

The first declares a function named **max** to be type double, the second declares **x_force** to be an array of ten single precision real numbers, the third declares a variable **x_coord** to be type float, and the last declares a variable **pi** to be type double. The exact range of values that may be represented by floating point objects is machine dependent.

2.2.2.1 float

Objects of type float are often stored in four bytes or 32 bits. If this is the case then values in the range from 10^{-38} to 10^{+38} may be represented. The numbers are represented internally in a binary or base two form. The 32 bits are broken up into 1 bit for the sign of the number, and an exponent and fractional part. The 8 bits for the exponent is represented as 1 bit for the sign of the exponent and 7 bits for the exponent. This gives a maximum exponent of 127 and 2^{127} is approximately 10^{+37}.

2.2.2.2 double

We expect objects of type double to require twice as much space as objects of type float. However, this depends upon the compiler. In some cases objects of type double may be stored in 8 bytes or 64 bits so that values in the range 10^{-308} to 10^{+308} may be represented. This gives greater precision or accuracy than float types. But some compilers use the same representation for objects of type double as for those of type float. In this case there is no difference in the range of values represented by double or float.

2.3 DERIVED TYPES

The arithmetic types of C are the basic or scalar types. We may declare and work with objects that are aggregates of objects of the scalar types. These are sometimes called "structured types." They consist of a collection of objects of the arithmetic types.

2.3.1 ARRAYS

An array is a sequence of objects, and each item in the sequence is of the same type. We may construct arrays of any type except for **void**. As an example consider int a[100]. Here we declare a to be an array consisting of 100 integers. The first element of the array is a[0] and the last element is a[99]. Generally if we make the declaration *type a[N]* then a is an array of *N* objects, each of type *type*. The first element of the array is a[0] and the last element is a[$N - 1$]. The range of subscripts for an array always go from 0 to 1 less than the size of an array.

Multidimensional arrays are arrays of arrays. To declare a two dimensional array bobo with 4 rows and 12 columns of numbers of type double we would write **double bobo[4] [12]**. The first element would be referenced by **bobo[0] [0]**, the second element is **bobo[0] [1]**, and the last element by **bobo[3] [11]**. Multidimensional arrays are stored row-by-row.

We may reference individual elements of an array by writing the array name followed by the appropriate subscript(s). Each of the elements has the type given in the declaration of the array. The array itself has a value associated with it as well. That value is the address of the array. So if we have the declaration **char ch[6]**, then ch[3] is of type char and represents a character. **ch** has as its value the address of an array or characters. From our discussions in the sections on character and string constants you may see that if we set ch[0] = 'H', ch[1] = 'e', ch[2] = 'l', ch[3] = 'l', ch[4] = 'o', and ch[5] = '\000', then ch represents the string "Hello".

2.3.2 POINTERS

A pointer holds the **address** of an object in memory or has the initial value 0 or NULL. So if we wanted p to hold the address of an integer (point to an integer) then we would make the declaration **int*p**. Pointers may point to objects of any type. The declaration **char*strs[10]**; identifiers **strs** as an array of pointers each of which points to a character.

If p is a pointer then the value of p is an address and *p is the object pointed to by p. Suppose that chp is a pointer to a character and that character is 'e'. Then chp has as its value the address of the character and *chp has 'e' as its value. As another example consider the following:

```
int x, y, *p;      /* declare x and y to be integers and p a pointer to
                       an integer */

p = &x;            /* assign the address of x, &x, to p so that p points
                       to x */

x = 4;             /* assign 4 to x */

y = *p;            /* assign the value of the object pointed to by p to y
                       that object is x, and its value is 4, so y has the
                       value 4 */

*p = 12;           /* assign 12 to the object pointed to by p that object
                       is x, so x now has the value 12 */
```

We may perform arithmetic on pointers. If p points to an object which occupies 4 bytes then p+8 points to an object of the same type as p and 32 bytes past p in memory. Similarly if p points to an object which occupies 10 bytes the p+8 points to an object of the same type 80 bytes past p in memory. Arithmetic with pointers is particularly appropriate when pointers and arrays are used together and is discussed in the next section.

2.3.3   POINTERS AND ARRAYS

Pointers and arrays have a great deal in common in C. Suppose xray is the name of an array. The object xray has the address of the first element of the array, xray[0], as its value. So if the elements of xray have type T, xray is a pointer to an object of type T. Remember that xray has as its value the address of xray[0], which may be written as &xray[0]. To be concrete suppose we have the following declarations:

```
float *fp, xray[10];.
```

Now it makes perfect sense to write fp = &xray[0]. That assigns the address of xray[0] to fp. That statement is equivalent to fp = xray for the reasons discussed above. From our comments on pointer arithmetic we know that fp + 2 points to an

15

object of type float and that it is located at the value of fp plus twice the size of a float object. But if fp holds the address of the xray[0] then fp + 2 refers to xray[2]. In this case fp+i is the address of xray[i] and *(fp+i) represents the contents of xray[i]. Likewise xray+i represents xray[i] and *(xray+i) represents the contents of xray[i]. Here is an example:

```
/* In this example x[i] is set to 3*i for i = 0 to 9.
    Then we set p to x (they're both addresses) and print
    the contents of x by changing the value of p.*/
    int *p, x[10], i;
    i = 0;
    while ( i < 10 ) {
            *(x + i) = i * 3;
            i++;
    }
    p = x;
    for (i = 0; i < 10; i ++) {
            printf(" The value of x[%d] is %d\n", i, *p);
            p = p + 1;
    }
/* Here the value in p is the address of x[9] */
/* Now we once again print the contents of x by using x as a
    pointer */
    for (i = 0); i < 10; i ++)
            printf(" The value of x[%d] is %d\n", i, *(x + i));
```

While arrays and pointers are similar they are not the same. A pointer is a variable while an array, that is, the address of an array, is a constant. In the example above we changed the value of p by writing p = p + 1. We could not do that with x. Putting the name of an array on the left of an assignment symbol, such as writing x = x + 1, implies that the address of the array would be changed. That's not possible. Likewise if x is the name of an array then x++, ++x, − −x, x− − is not allowed, but if p is a pointer then those prefix and postfix operators may be applied to p.

2.3.4 FUNCTIONS

Functions are executable code but they do have a type associated with them. The type of the function is declared when the function is declared. For example,

void greet (char *) double cubroot (double) char *t (char *)

are declarations of functions. The second will return a value of type double, the third a value of type pointer to char, and the first returns no value. It is also possible to define a pointer to a function. This is useful for the cases in which a function is an argument to another function.

2.3.5 STRUCTURES

A structure in C is a data object similar to a record in COBOL or Pascal. It consists of several objects, each of which must be named and each may be a different type. Recall that each object in an array must be of the same type so that an array is termed homogeneous. A structure may be a heterogeneous collection of objects.

An example is

```
struct student {
        char name[30];
        long int idnum;
        float gpa;
}
```

This is not a variable but the form of a structure named student; student is called the structure tag. We can declare variables as struct student me, class473[30], *top;. Here me is a structure of the form of student, class473 is an array of thirty structures, and top is a pointer to a structure of form student. Also me.name is how we refer to the name field of me, class473[6].idnum is the idnum field of the seventh element of class473, and either top-> gpa or (*top).gpa refers to the gpa field of the object pointed to by top.

Structures may also be used to refer to individual bits of objects. In this case we say they are bit fields. For example

```
struct exmpl { int sbit:1; int rbyte:7; int mbits:20; int lnibble:4}
```

followed by struct exmpl forbytes; allows us to refer to the first bit of forbytes as forbytes.sbit, the next seven bits as forbytes.rbyte, and so on.

2.3.6 UNIONS

A union in C is similar to a "variant record" in Pascal. Its form and syntax is the same as for structures. However, the implementation is different. Only one of the fields is present in memory at any one time. For example union varitype { int ival; float rval; char cval; } defines a union structure whose tag is varitype. A variable of this type is declared as **union varitype invar**. We may refer to invar.ival, invar.rval, or inval.cval. Each of these refer to the same memory location and are interpreted as integer, floating point, or char respectively. The compiler allocates the maximum necessary space when the program is translated. The union type is useful, but can also lead to problems unless care is used.

2.4 CONVERSIONS FROM ONE TYPE TO ANOTHER

Type conversions are a usual and normal part of most languages. Consider **int i, x; float y; x = 23; y = 12.3; i = x + y;**. Since x and y are different types one must be converted to perform the addition. In C, as in most languages, the value in x is temporarily converted to float and the result of the addition is 35.3. This value must be stored into the location named i which is type int, so that another conversion must take place. Here the result of the addition is converted to 35 and stored in the location named i. This was a relatively simple case.

Type conversion and its rules may get very complicated as

it sometimes depends on the particular implementation of the compiler and representation of data objects. However, we expect the "law of least astonishment" to hold. We expect to preserve the original value whenever possible. If the new type cannot represent the original value then we expect as best an approximation as possible. C is not as strict about enforcing type compatibility as other languages, such as Pascal. Wherever possible type conversions are performed.

We have been discussing implicit conversions performed by the languages system. A programmer may provide instructions for explicit conversions through the use of the **cast** expressions.

2.4.1 PROMOTIONS

In order to reduce the number of operators necessary to perform computations some types are "widened" or "promoted" to types that can represent all the values of the original type.

Original	Promoted to
char, short	int
unsigned char	unsigned
unsigned short	unsigned
float	double
'array of'	'pointer to'
'function returning'	'pointer to function returning'

2.4.2 ARITHMETIC CONVERSIONS

Some conversions are performed to allow for arithmetic calculations as discussed above. Here are rules governing necessary conversions.

1. If one operand is type **double**, then the other operand is converted to type **double**.

2. Otherwise, if one operand is type **unsigned long int,** the other

19

is converted to **unsigned long int.**

3. Otherwise, if one operand is type **long int,** and the other operand is type **unsigned int,** then each of the two operands is converted to type **unsigned long int.**

4. Otherwise, if one operand is of type **long int,** then the other operand (necessarily of type int) is converted to type **long int.**

5. Otherwise if one operand is of type **unsigned int,** then the other is converted to type **unsigned int.**

2.4.3 OTHER CONVERSIONS

When floating point objects are converted to integer objects the fractional part is discarded. It may happen that the floating point value is beyond the range of representable integer values. In that case the result is not specified. It may result in an overflow exception or a value that has no meaningful relation to the original value.

There are a number of other cases to consider, such as conversion from one type of floating point type to another, from one type of integer type (remember there are six) to another, and so on. The reader should consult a reference book on C for these details.

2.4.4 CAST

Any legal type conversion can be forced by the use of an operator called a **cast** (a type cast). The general form is

(type) expression

For example, the function **log** (part of the math library) calculates the natural logarithm of its argument and it expects an argument of type double. If we have declared **int x** and wish to calculate the natural log of x we may do so by casting x to type double as follows: **log ((double) x).** Here are some other valid casts:

```
int i, *intp;
char ch, *charp;
float rr;
enum c { red, blue, yellow } primary;
•

•

intp = (int*) charp;
cp = (char*) intp;
i = (int) primary;
rr = (float) log( (double) ( (int) *charp ) );
primary = (enum c) ( (int) rr);
•

•
```

CHAPTER 3

EXPRESSIONS

3.1 EXPRESSION DEFINITIONS

Expressions provide a means for manipulating variables and constants. They are made up of identifiers and operators.

3.1.1 OBJECTS AND LVALUES

A data object is a portion of memory that is treated as a unit by a program. The objects may be examined and/or modified. Objects that can be modified are called **lvalues**. They get their name from the fact that if a variable is an **lvalue** then it may appear on the left of an assignment operator. The declaration **int abc[10]**; declares abc as the name of an array. It is an object, of ten integers, each of which is an object. It is not possible to place abc to the left of an assignment operator since the "value" of abc is the address of the array. However, the expression **a[4] = 23;** is a valid expression. While the array is not an lvalue, each of the elements of the array are. Likewise **a[4+1]** is an lvalue, but **a[4] + 1** is not. Some expressions are lvalues while others are not. As we discuss operators and expressions we will indicate whether each is an lvalue.

3.2 PRECEDENCE AND ASSOCIATIVITY OF OPERATORS

The operators of C were given in section 1.5. Here we present them in order of their precedence, from highest to lowest, along with their associativity.

Operators	Associativity
() [] − > .	left to right[1]
! ~ ++ − − + − * & (type) sizeof	right to left[2]
* / %	left to right
+ −	left to right
< < > >	left to right
< <= > >=	left to right
= = !=	left to right
&	left to right
^	left to right
|	left to right
&&	left to right
||	left to right
?:	right to left
= += − = *= /= %= &= ^= |= <<= >>=	right to left
,	left to right

(1) () includes function calls and parenthesized expressions
(2) +, −, * indicate unary operators

3.3 PRIMARY EXPRESSIONS

There are four kinds of primary expressions: identifier or name, constant or literal, string, and parenthesized expressions of the form (**expression**).

3.3.1 IDENTIFIER PRIMARY EXPRESSION

A declared identifier or name is a primary expression. The type of a primary expression is the declared type of the identi-

23

fier. It is an **lvalue** if the identifier is declared to be arithmetic, pointer, enumeration, structure, or union type. Array names and function names are not lvalues.

3.3.2 CONSTANT PRIMARY EXPRESSIONS

A constant or string literal is a primary expression. It evaluates to an object of the type of the constant. For example, 34.67 is a literal which evaluates to type double or float and "Hello" is a string constant which evaluates to an array of char or a pointer to char. Constant primary expressions are not lvalues.

3.3.3 PARENTHESIZED EXPRESSIONS

A parenthesized expression consists of a left parenthesis, followed by any expression, and followed by a right parenthesis. The value of the parenthesized expression is the value of the expression within the parentheses. If the expression within the parentheses is an lvalue then so is the parenthesized expression.

3.4 POSTFIX EXPRESSIONS

Postfix expressions are

subscripted expressions – expressions that contain a subscript such as references to array elements,

function call expressions – the expressions used to call a function,

component selection expressions – those used to reference a member of a structure or a union, and

postincrement or **postdecrement expressions** – those used to increase or decrease the value of an expression after it has been evaluated.

3.4.1 SUBSCRIPTED EXPRESSIONS

A subscripted expression is an expression followed by another expression enclosed in square brackets, e.g., temps[1+w].

Such expressions are used to refer to a single element of an array. The expression outside of the brackets must be the name of an array or evaluate to the address of the beginning of an array. The expression inside the brackets must be an expression of type integer. The postfix expression **a[i]** is evaluated as ***(a + i)**. Recall that **a** holds the address of **a[0]** and we are referencing the ith element past the beginning of the array. Since we are accessing array elements the expression within the brackets must evaluate to an integer. Since **a[i]** is the same as ***(a + i)** array subscripts must start with the value 0. Elements of multi-dimensional arrays are referenced by subscripted expressions. For example: **shelves [2] [34]** references the 34th element of the 2nd row of the two-dimensional array shelves. Subscripted expressions are lvalues.

3.4.2 FUNCTION CALL EXPRESSIONS

A function may be called or invoked by an expression of the form

function-name (argument-list)

That is, a function name followed by a list of zero or more arguments enclosed in parentheses. Commas are used to separate the arguments. Some examples are: **fun1()**, **odd(x)**, **simpstat(data, mean, var, num-1)**, **xchange(&g,&h)** and **dotprod (x,z[3])**. The function fun1 has no arguments, odd has one argument, and the others have several. Naturally the order of the arguments must match the list of parameters in the function definition or declaration. The arguments may be evaluated in any order. Assume i equals 5. On one machine it may be that funy(i,i++) has the same effect as writing funy(5,5) while on another it may be equivalent to the function call f(5,6).

Since functions may be (and often are) compiled separately, it is important to declare functions. That way the compiler can check for the proper number, type and order of arguments for each function call.

The arguments to a function are evaluated when the function expression is executed. Only the values of the arguments, the result of this evaluation, are passed to the function. All arguments are thus passed by value. Functions may modify array elements if the address of the array – the name of the array or a pointer to the array – is an argument. The values held in other variables may be modified by a function if it receives the address of that variable. In one example above we used &g and &h as xchange modifies the values in g and h.

3.4.3 STRUCTURE MEMBER AND UNION MEMBER EXPRESSIONS

A structure or a union is a data object with a number of components of possibly different types. The operators . and –> are used to select the components.

Consider the declaration

```
struct student {
        char name[30];
        long int idnum;
        float gpa;
}
struct student me, *top, class473[30];
```

We can select or refer to the second component of each of the first two variables as **me.idnum** or **top–>idnum**. Since **class473** is an array, each of its elements **class473[0]** thru **class473[29]** is a structure. Each of these has a second component and they may be referred to or selected as **class473[0].idnum**, **class473[1].idnum**, ..., **class473[29].idnum**. The form for member selection from a structure or union is

   postfix-expression.identifier or postfix-expression–>identifier.

The operator –> is used if the postfix-expression to its left is a pointer. **me.idnum** and **(&me)–>idnum** are both valid references to the same object. The format for member selection expressions for unions is the same as for structures. These ex-

26

pressions are lvalues if the first expression is an lvalue and the expression following the . or –> is not an array.

3.4.4 POSTFIX INCREMENT AND DECREMENT

A postfix expression which is also an lvalue can be evaluated and then incremented (++) or decremented (– –) by expressions of the form

operand ++ **or** *operand – –*

The value of the postfix increment or decrement expression is the value of the operand. After the operand is evaluated it is incremented (++) or decremented (– –). That is why the operand must be an lvalue and also why an expression of this form is not an lvalue.

Consider the following program.

```
#include <stdio.h>
main(void)
{
 /* declare identifiers */
    int pfex, aray[10], *p;
 /* initialize first three elements of aray, pfex, and p */
    aray[0] = aray[1] = aray[2] = 0;
    pfex = 1;
    p = aray;
 /* set aray[pfex] to 9 */
    aray[pfex] = 9;
 /* print pfex, first three elements of aray, and *p */
    printf(" pfex = %d, aray[0] = %d, aray[1] = %d, aray [2] = %d,
        *p = %d\n", pfex, aray[0], aray[1], aray[2], *p);
 /* set aray[pfex] to 5 and decrement pfex */
    aray[pfex– –] = 5;
 /* increment aray[pfex] */
    aray[pfex] ++;
 /* print pfex, first three elements of aray, and *p */
    printf(" pfex = %d, aray[0] = %d, aray[1] = %d, aray [2] = %d,
        *p = %d\n", pfex, aray[0], aray[1], aray[2], *p);
```

27

```
/* increment object pointed to by p */
    (*p)++;
/* print pfex, first three elements of aray, and *p */
    printf(" pfex = %d, aray[0] = %d, aray[1] = %d, aray [2] = %d,
        *p = %d\n", pfex, aray[0], aray[1], aray[2], *p);
/* increment p */
    p ++;
/* print pfex, first three elements of aray, and *p */
    printf(" pfex = %d, aray[0] = %d, aray[1] = %d, aray [2] = %d,
        *p = %d\n", pfex, aray[0], aray[1], aray[2], *p);
}
```

Here is the output of the program.

```
pfex = 1, array[0] = 0, array[1] = 9, array[2] = 0, *p = 0
pfex = 0, array[0] = 1, array[1] = 5, array[2] = 0, *p = 1
pfex = 0, array[0] = 2, array[1] = 5, array[2] = 0, *p = 2
pfex = 0, array[0] = 2, array[1] = 5, array[2] = 0, *p = 5
```

Initially **pfex** is one, **aray[1]** has been set to 9, and ***p**– the object to which **p** points – has the value 0, the value of **a[0]**. After the statement **aray[pfex– –]=5** is executed **array[1] is set to 5** and **pfex** is decremented. The statement **(*p)++** increments the value pointed to by **p** and **p** still has the address of the array or the location of **array[0]** as its value. After this the value of **aray[0]** is modified. Finally, the expression **p++** modifies the value of **p. p** is incremented so it has the address of **aray[1]** as its value.

3.5 UNARY EXPRESSIONS

Unary expressions are expressions with one operator and one operand. They have lower precedence than postfix expressions but higher than any binary expression. For example ***p++** is equivalent to ***(p ++)** and different than **(*p)++**. Postfix expressions are considered unary expressions. The other unary expressions are:

Type	Form
preincrement expressions	++ operand
predecrement expressions	– – operand
indirection expression	*operand
address expression	&operand
unary plus	+operand
unary minus	–operand
logical negation	!operand
bitwise compliment	~operand
sizeof expression	sizeof(type-name) or sizeof(operand)

3.5.1 PREINCREMENT (++) AND PREDECREMENT (– –) EXPRESSIONS

A preincrement expression has the form **++operand**. It is evaluated by incrementing the operand. The value of the preincrement expression is the value of operand after it has been incremented. Since operand is modified it must be an lvalue and it must be a scalar type. The preincrement expression is not an lvalue. Predecrement expressions are treated in the same way except that operand is decremented. For example:

```
#include <stdio.h>
main (void)
{
        int a, b, c;
        a = 5; b = 10;
        printf(" a = %d, b = %d\n", a, b);
        ++a; – – b;
        printf(" a = %d, b = %d\n", a, b);
        a = ++a – – – b;
        printf(" a = %d, b = %d\n", a, b);
}
```

produces the output

```
a = 5, b = 10
a = 6, b = 9
a = – 1, b = 8
```

29

3.5.2 INDIRECTION EXPRESSIONS

An **indirect expression** has the form *operand. They are used to reference the object pointed to by a pointer. For example, if p is a pointer to an object of type int then *p is the integer. The indirect expression is an lvalue if the pointer points to an lvalue. If p is a pointer to a function then *p is a function. If p is a null pointer or otherwise undefined then *p yields an unpredictable result. Otherwise, an indirection expression *operand returns the object to which operand points.

3.5.3 ADDRESS EXPRESSIONS

Address expressions are of the form &operand. This yields the address of operand. operand must be function type, an lvalue which does not refer to a bit-field, or an lvalue which does not refer to an object whose storage class is register. If operand has type T then &operand is a pointer to an object of type T. For example if prex is of type int then &prex is the address of prex and so is a pointer to an integer. Also *(&prex) is the equivalent to prex.

3.5.4 UNARY PLUS AND UNARY MINUS

The operand to unary plus (+) and unary minus (–) must be arithmetic. The result of applying + to an operand is the value of the operand and applying – to an operand yields the negative of the operand. Some examples are

–b + a, +b * –a, and –(*p)++.

In the first we add the negative of b to a, in the second we multiply b by the negative of a, and in the third we reference the object pointed to by p, increment it, and then evaluate the negative of it. An expression of this form is not an lvalue.

3.5.5 LOGICAL NEGATION

The operator ! may be applied to any scalar type or any pointer. If x is a scalar type then !x evaluates to 0 if x is not

30

zero and it evaluates to 1 otherwise. If x is a pointer then !x evaluates to 1 if x is a null pointer and 0 otherwise. Regardless of the type of x, !x is type int. An expression of this form is not an lvalue.

3.5.6 BITWISE COMPLEMENT

The operator ~ is used to obtain the bitwise compliment of an integral object. For each bit in the representation of, say, x, if the bit is 1, then the same bit will be 0 in ~x and if the bit is 0 then the same bit will be 1 in ~x. If x is unsigned int, ~x yields **UINT_MAX −x**. Where **UINT_MAX** is the largest unsigned integer represented by the language system. For example, if a program contains

```
unsigned int x;
x = 10;
printf(" x = %u, ~x = %u\n", x ~x);
```

then we obtain **x = 10 ~x = 65525** as output on a particular system. This indicates that the largest value for an unsigned int is 65535 and that 16 bits are used to represent an integer.

3.5.7 SIZEOF

Sizeof gives the number of bytes required to store its operand. If x is type char then **sizeof x** returns 1. If x were a structure, then sizeof x would return the number of bytes necessary to store x. Sizeof may not be applied to a function or a bit-field operand. Sizeof may be used to determine the number of elements of an array. If aray is an array then **(sizeof aray)/(sizeof aray[0])** is the number of elements in aray.

3.6 CAST EXPRESSIONS

A cast expression has the form **(type-name) expression**. It converts the type of one expression to another type. For example,

```
(int) (23.45 + a)
```

converts 23.45 +a to a value of type int. Cast has been discussed in more detail in section 2.4.4. An expression with a cast is not an lvalue.

3.7 MULTIPLICATIVE EXPRESSIONS

Multiplicative expressions are binary expressions, evaluated from left to right, and have precedence immediately below that of unary expressions. The operators used in multiplicative expressions are

*	multiplication
/	division
%	remainder or modulus

3.7.1 MULTIPLICATION EXPRESSIONS

Multiplication expressions have the form **operand1* operand2**. Each operand must have arithmetic type and the usual conversions are performed. Multiplication is assumed to be commutative and associative. A compiler is free to interpret the order of calculation so that the expression **a*(s*c)*t** may be evaluated as **(c*a)*(s*t)**. It is wise not to write expressions that depend upon the order of evaluation.

3.7.2 DIVISION EXPRESSIONS

Division expressions have the form **operand1 / operand2**. Each operand must have arithmetic type and the usual conversions are performed. The / has its usual arithmetic meaning if both operands are floating type. If both operands are integer type then the expression results in some truncation or rounding. If both operands are positive and the division doesn't yield a whole number then the result is truncated. For example,

```
#include <stdio.h>
main (void)
```

```
{
        int x, y, z;
        x = 35; y = 4;
        printf(" x = %4d, y = %4d; x/y = %4d \n", x, y, x/y);
        x = -x;
        printf(" x = %4d, y = %4d; x/y = %4d \n", x, y, x/y);
        y = -y;
        printf(" x = %4d, y = %4d; x/y = %4d \n", x, y, x/y);
}
```

yields

```
x =  35, y =  4; x/y =  8
x = -35, y =  4; x/y = -8
x = -35, y = -4; x/y =  8
```

Truncation occurred when neither, one, or both operands were negative. If one operand is negative the result is implementation dependent.

3.7.3   REMAINDER OR MODULUS EXPRESSIONS

The division operator (/) yields the quotient of when both operands are integral type. The remainder operator (%) yields the remainder. Since 4 divides 35 eight times with a remainder of 3, we have $35/4 = 8$ and $35\%4 = 3$.

If b is not 0 then it is always true that $(a/b)*b + a\%b$ is equal to a.

If both a and b are non-negative then a%b is less than b. If one is negative then the absolute value of a%b is less than the absolute value of b.

3.8   ADDITIVE EXPRESSIONS

Additive expressions are binary expressions, evaluated from left to right, and have precedence immediately below multiplicative expressions. The operators used in additive expressions are

```
+        addition
-        subtraction.
```

3.8.1 ADDITION EXPRESSIONS

Addition expressions have the form **operand1 + operand2**. If both operands are numeric then it evaluates to the sum of the operands. A pointer into an array and any integral type may be added. If **p** is a pointer then **p + j** points to an object j times (sizeof*p) bytes past p in memory. So if aray is an array and **p = &aray[i]** then **p + j** is the address of **aray[i + j]**. Also ***(p+j)** references the value of **aray[i + j]**. If the resulting addition of a pointer into an array and an integer yields a value outside the bounds of the array then the result may be undefined. Only if the sum is one past the end of the array is the result defined. For example if we have the program fragment

```
int aray[10], *p;
p = aray;
```

then a reference of **p+10** is valid or defined while **p+11** may not be valid.

3.8.2 SUBTRACTION EXPRESSIONS

A subtraction expression has the form **operand1 − operand2**. If both operands are numeric then it evaluates to the difference of the operands. A pointer into an array and any integral type may be subtracted. Also one pointer may be subtracted from another provided that they point to objects in the same array. Otherwise the result may not be defined. For example if we have the program fragment

```
int aray[10], *p, *q;
p = aray;
q = p + 9;
```

then $q - p$ is equal to 9. Also $p + (q - p)/2$ points to aray[4].

3.9   BITWISE SHIFT EXPRESSIONS

The operators **>>** and **<<** shift the bits of an integer right or left, respectively. Bitwise shift expressions have the form **operand1 >> operand2** or **operand 1 << operand2**. Both operands must be one of the integral types. Appropriate promotions take place. If operand2, the expression on the right, is negative or greater than or equal to the number of bits of the operand on the left then the result is undefined. If operand1 is unsigned then all vacated bits are filled with zeros. Otherwise, all vacated bits except for the sign bit are filled with zeros. Octal representation of an integer is used in the place of operand1 in the following examples.

001062 >> 3 yields 000106   001062 << 3 yields 010620

3.10   RELATIONAL EXPRESSIONS

Relational expressions are used for comparison of the values of expressions. The relational operators are

<	less than	>	greater than
<=	less than or equal	>=	greater than or equal.

The result of a relational expression is either 1, if the relation is true, or 0 otherwise. The operands to a relational expression must be either both arithmetic or both pointer types. If pointers are used they must point into the same array. Appropriate promotions or conversions are performed to evaluate the relational expression. Below we make remarks concerning the operator >. Similar remarks hold for each of the operators.

Consider the expression p > q. Suppose p is unsigned int and q is int. During the evaluation of the expression, q will be promoted to unsigned. If q is negative then as the result of the promotion it will be interpreted as a very large value. It is better to write (signed int) p > q.

Expressions of the form a > b > c are valid, but are not evaluated in the usual mathematical sense. The expression is evaluated from left to right. If it happens that a is greater than b then a > b will result in a value of 1. Then the expression 1 > c is evaluated. The operator &&, discussed below, can be used to determine if a > b and b > c.

3.11 EQUALITY EXPRESSIONS

Equality expressions use the operators == and !=. The operators are binary operators. As in the case of relational expressions, a value of 1 is returned if the expression is true and 0 otherwise. These operators are at a lower level of precedence than the relational operators. The usual conversions are performed. If we have the following program fragment

```
int x;
float y;
char a;
/* store the character 'f' in a */
a = 'f';
/* store 102, the ASCII code for 'f', in x */
x = 102;
/* store 102.0 in y */
y = 102.0
```

we can expect that a == x, a == y, and y == x each evaluate to 1. These operators may also be used to compare pointers. Be aware that the expression operand1 == operand2 is much different that operand1 = operand2. The former is used to determine if the two operands have the same value while the latter is an assignment statement which causes a modification of operand1.

3.12 BITWISE *AND* EXPRESSIONS

Bitwise AND expressions have the form **operand1 & operand2**. Both operands must be integral and the usual conversions are performed. The result of the operation is another object of integral type in which each bit is 1 if the corresponding bits in both operands were 1, and 0 otherwise. Since the binary representation for twelve is 1100 and the binary representation for ten is 1010, 12 & 10 yields eight whose binary representation is 1000. If we use octal representation then 02061 & 02345 results in 02041. If a, b, and c are integral types and a is greater than b, and b is greater than c then a > b & b > c evaluates to 1. The bitwise AND is sometimes referred to as a "masking operation." For example we may determine the contents of the 4 rightmost bits of x by evaluating x & 017.

The operation & is commutative and associative. An expression of the form **(c & s) & (a & t)** may be evaluated **(c & a) & (s & t)**.

3.13 Bitwise eXclusive *OR* EXPRESSIONS

Bitwise eXclusive OR expressions have the form **operand1 ^ operand2**. Both operands must be integral and the usual conversions are performed. The result of the operation is another object of integral type in which each bit is 1 if the corresponding bits in both operands were different, and 0 if they were the same. This is sometimes called an **exclusive or** operation. Since the binary representation for twelve is 1100 and the binary representation for ten is 1010, 12 ^ 10 yields six whose binary representation is 0110. If we use octal representation then 02061 ^ 02345 results in 00324.

The operation ^ is commutative and associative. An expression of the form **(c ^ s) ^ (a ^ t)** may be evaluated **(c ^ a) ^ (s ^ t)**.

3.14 Bitwise *OR* EXPRESSIONS

Bitwise OR expressions have the form **operand1 | operand2**. Both operands must be integral and the usual conversions are performed. The result of the operation is another object of integral type in which each bit is 1 if the corresponding bits in either operand were a one, and 0 if they both were zero. Since the binary representation for twelve is 1100 and the binary representation for ten is 1010, 12 | 10 yields fourteen whose binary representation is 1110. If we use octal representation then 02061 | 02345 results in 02365.

The operation | is commutative and associative. An expression of the form **(c | s) | (a | t)** may be evaluated **(c | a) | (s | t)**.

3.15 LOGICAL *AND* (&&) and *OR* (||) EXPRESSIONS

There are two logical operators:

&& AND || OR

The operator **&&** has a higher precedence than the operator | |. These logical expressions are evaluated to the point that the outcome may be determined. In an expression of the form **operand1 && operand2**, if operand1 evaluates to 0, then operand2 is not evaluated. In an expression of the form **operand1 | | operand2**, if operand1 evaluates to 1 then operand 2 is not evaluated. In other words, an AND expression is evaluated until one of the operands is false, and an OR expression is evaluated until one of the expressions is true.

3.15.1 LOGICAL *AND* (&&) EXPRESSIONS

Logical AND expressions have the form **operand1 && operand2**. The operands may be of any scalar type. The result is type int and has value either 0 or 1. If both operands are nonzero then the result is 1. If at least one of the operands is 0 then the result is 0. The operands are evaluated from left to right until each evaluates to a non-zero value or until one evaluates to zero. In the following example we expect output of

```
len = 4
q = .55d, len = 4
len = 10
```

```
#include <stdio.h>
static char*qa[ ] = {"1234.55d", "hello world"};
main (void)
{
    char p, *q;
    int i, l, len;
    p = '.';
    i = 0;
    while ( i < 2 ) {
        q = qa[i++];
        len = 0;

        while ( p! = *q&&*(++q)!= '\0')
          len++;

        printf("len = %d \n",len);
        if (*q != '\0')
            printf( "q = %s, len = %d \n",q, len);
    }
}
```

At the second **while** statement we are evaluating the expression

    p != *q &&*(++q)!= '\0'

If it happens that ***q == p**, as it does with the first string, then we do not evaluate *(++q)!= '\0' so that **q** points to the character '.' in the string. Otherwise, when *q != p, we evaluate the expression following **&&** and modify **q**.

3.15.2 LOGICAL *OR* (| |) EXPRESSIONS

Logical OR expressions have the form **operand1 | | operand2.** The operands may be of any scalar type. The result is type int and has value either 0 or 1. If both operands are zero then the result is 0. If at least one of the operands is non-zero then the result is 1. The operands are evaluated from left to right until all are evaluated or one evaluates to a non-zero value. In the following example we expect output of

```
x = 1, y = -3, z = 4, i = 1
x = 2, y = -2, z = 5, i = 2
x = 3, y = -1, z = 6, i = 3
x = 4, y =  0, z = 7, i = 4
x = 5, y =  1, z = 8, i = 5
x = 6, y =  2, z = 9, i = 6
x = 7, y =  3, z = 10, i = 7
x = 8, y =  4, z = 11, i = 8
```

```
main (void)
{
    int i, x, y, z;
    x = 1; y = -3; z = 4;
    for ( i = 1; x < 5 || y < 5 || z < 5; i++)
        printf("x=%d, y=%d, z=%d, i = %d\n", x++, y++,z++,i);
}
```

The logical OR expression

```
x < 5 || y < 5 || z < 5
```

controls the **for** loop. As long as it evaluates to 1 the loop continues. We exit the loop only when all three variables, x, y, and z, have a value greater than or equal to 5.

3.16 CONDITIONAL EXPRESSIONS

Conditional expressions have the form

```
expression1 ? expression2 : expression3
```

The expression (x >= 0) ? x: -x is an example. If **expression1** evaluates to zero then **expression3** is evaluated, otherwise **ex-**

pression2 is evaluated. The first expression must be a scalar type – it is often a logical expression. The others may be of various types, provided they are of the same type. Exactly one of **expression2** or **expression3** is evaluated. The type of the result is the type of **expression2** or **expression3**. The expression in the example above evaluates the absolute value of x. If x is greater than or equal to 0 then the expression returns x, otherwise it returns the negative of x.

3.17 ASSIGNMENT EXPRESSIONS

C offers several assignment operators. They are

`=    +=    —=    *=    /=    %=    >>=    <<=    &=    ^=    |=`

and incorporate previous operators. An assignment expression has the form

lvalue assignment-operator expression

The lvalue to the left of assignment-operator is modified as a result. The assignment expression has the value of the modified lvalue as its value. For example, the expression

`a = 23 + ( x = 12 )`

gives **a** the value 35, after it has assigned **x** the value 12. The expression has the value 35. For another example consider **x = y = z = 0**; which initializes x, y, and z to 0.

3.17.1 SIMPLE ASSIGNMENT

Simple assignment expressions have the form

lvalue = expression

The lvalue is modified to the value of the expression to the right of =. The assignment expression has the value of the lvalue as its value. For example in

`a[i] = b + (c – (d = 3) ) + 2`

we first assign 3 to d, then subtract 3 from c, add the result to d and 2, and then modify a[i]. Also consider

```
if ( a[i] = b + (c − (d = 3) ) + 2 )
    printf ("OK so far \n");
```

If the expression to the right of = is zero then the printf will not be executed.

Expressions such as aray[v++] = v should be avoided. The order of evaluation of v is not specified.

3.17.2 COMPOUND ASSIGNMENT

Compound assignment statements involve another operation with assignment. They have the form

lvalue op = expression

They are equivalent to

lvalue = lvalue op expression

For example xlval *= 3 is equivalent to xlval = xlval * 3. The lvalue is evaluated only once. So while xlval% = 10 is equivalent to xlval = xlval % 10, aray[i++] − = 12 is not equivalent to aray[i++] = aray[i++] − 12.

3.18 COMMA EXPRESSIONS

These expressions are made up of expressions separated by one comma for every pair of expressions. The comma indicates sequential evaluation. The expression pi = 3.14, diam = 2*pi*r, area = diam*r/2; is an example. The expressions are evaluated left to right. As an expression is evaluated its value is discarded. The value of the rightmost expression is the value of the comma expression. So in our example the expression has value of area. First pi is initialized, then diam is computed, and finally area.

42

Here is an example which prints the elements of an array in two columns after filling it in a silly way.

```
main (void)
{
    int xray[20], x, y;
    for ( x = 0; x < 20; x++)
        xray [x] = ( x%5)? x : -x;
    for (x = 0, y = 10; x < 10; x++, y++)
        printf(" %3d \t\t %3d\n",xray[x], xray[y]);
}
```

The output is

0	-10
1	11
2	12
3	13
4	14
-5	-15
6	16
7	17
8	18
9	19

3.19 CONSTANT EXPRESSIONS

Constant expressions can only be expressions that can be calculated at compile time, when the program is being translated. An example would be the expression

(sizeof aray) / (sizeof aray[0])

The evaluation of a constant expression at compile time must yield the same result as if it were evaluated during execution. Several different forms of expressions are allowed provided that all may be done while the program is being translated. Any information that is dynamic, not known until execution, may not be used. Constant expressions may not contain assignments, increments, decrements, function calls, or comma operators except as part of the operand of sizeof. Each item in an operand of a constant expression that is not used with sizeof, must be integral type or cast to a specific integral type.

CHAPTER 4

STATEMENTS

Statements control the flow of execution in a program. There are three fundamental control structures to specify the order of execution in a C program. They are

sequential control	the next statement is executed
conditional control	one statement out of several possible is executed
iterative control	a block of statements are executed repeatedly

In addition to using these control structures, there is a group of statements used to transfer the flow of control of execution from one point to another. C contains the assortment of statements one normally expects to find in a modern programming language. Statements are constructed from expressions. However, an expression has a value associated with it and a statement has no value.

The term "statement" will refer to a single simple statement or a compound, block statement.

4.1   EXPRESSION STATEMENTS

Expression statements are simple statements and have the form **expression;** some examples are

```
a = b + c; d++; *s++ = *++t; number %= 10;
( class– >studt.grade >= 60 ) ? pass++ : fail++;
```

4.2 COMPOUND STATEMENTS

A **compound statement** is also called a **block**. A compound statement has the form

```
{
    statement1
    statement2
    •
    •
    statementn
}
```

The character { starts a block, and } ends a block. These characters enclose a sequence of statements. Every function contains at least one block. Any declarations made within a block are in effect within that block and any block contained within. The following program fragment

```
{
    int x, y;
    x = 0; y = 0;
    printf(" Outer block: x = %d, y = %d\n, x, y);
    {
        int y;
        y = 1; x = y++ *3;
        printf(" Inner block: x = %d, y = %d \n, x, y);
    }
    printf(" Outer block: x = %d, y = %d\n, x, y);
}
```

would produce the output

```
Outerblock: x = 0, y = 0
Inner block: x = 6, y = 1
Outerblock: x = 6, y = 0
```

This is because the object named y in the inner block is different than the object named y in the outer block. There is only

46

one object named x in either block. A variable may be referenced only if it has been declared within a block or in a block enclosing the present block.

4.3   SELECTION STATEMENTS

Selection statements provide conditional control for C programs. They are the IF statement and the SWITCH statement. The first is used to select according to some condition, one of two statements to be executed. The SWITCH statement is similar to a CASE statement in other languages and is used to select one of several statements or statement blocks.

4.3.1   *IF* STATEMENT

An IF statement has the form

    if (expression) statement1;

or the form

    if (expression) statement1 else statement2;

In either case **expression** is evaluated. If its value is not zero then it is taken to be "true" and statement1 is executed. If expression evaluates to zero then it is taken to be "false." In the first case statement1 is not executed. In the second case statement2 is executed. The else always goes with the most recent if, unless that if is within a block.

Some examples are

```
/* example 1*/
    if ( top == 0 )
        printf(" Empty \n" );

/* example 2 */
    if ( top == 0 )
        return (0);
    else {
        request ( nexttok );
```

47

```
        process (nexttok );
        if ( nexttok > base ) count++;
        push ( nexttok );
    }
/* example 3 */
    if ( ( linin = getline ( fp, MAX ) ) != NULL ) {
        lincnt++;
        if ( lincnt > pglnth )
            pgnum++;
    }
    else
        display ( text );
```

The first example is a simple **if** statement. If top is equal to zero
then Empty and a new line character are sent to the standard
output file. In example 2, if top evaluates to 0 then a return
statement with a value of 0 is executed. Otherwise a compound
statement is executed. The third example evaluates the expression (**linin = getline(fp, MAX)) != NULL.** As an aside, this
expression is evaluated by calling a function getline with two
arguments, assigning the result of that function to linin, and
then determining if the value returned is NULL. If the expression evaluates to 1 then we enter a block to execute the compound statement. The else refers to the outer **if** statement because the inner **if** is enclosed in a block. In this case the **if**
statement within the compound statement is invisible to the
else.

4.3.2   *SWITCH* STATEMENT

The SWITCH statement is used to select one statement
from several alternatives. It is similar to the CASE statement in
Pascal and Ada. However, its syntax and implementation is
somewhat different. The SWITCH statement has the form

```
switch (expression) {
    case constant-expression1:                    statement 1;
    case constant-expression2:                    statement 2;
        •
```

```
          case constant-expressionk:                                    statementk;
          default:              statementd
}
```

The keyword **switch** begins the statement. An expression is
evaluated and compared with each of the constant expressions
following the keyword **case**. Each of these constant expressions must evaluate to different values. If a match is made then
the corresponding statement is executed. If no match is made
and there is a label **default**, then the statement following the
keyword **default** is executed. If no match is made then the
statement following the terminating } of the switch is executed.
Additionally, if a match is made then all statements to the
terminating } of the switch are executed. If only the statement
corresponding to a particular constant-expression is to be executed then a **break;** statement must be included. Here is an
example.

```
enum days { sun, mon, tue, wed, thu, fri, sat } today;

    switch ( today ) {
        case sun:;
        case sat: printf (" Weekend !! \n");
            break;
        case mon:;
        case wed:;                                                ;
        case fri:printf(" Programming Languages Class at
            10:00 \n");
            break;
        case tue:                    printf(" Department Seminar \n");
            break;
        case thu:                    printf(" Committee Meeting \n");
            break;
        default: printf(" ERROR \b \b ");
            printf(" %d – value in switch \n", today);
    }
```

In the example we take the same action if today evaluates to
sun or sat. Likewise if it evaluates to mon, wed, or fri. Separate

actions are taken on tue and thu. The default label marks action to be taken if none of the other values were matched.

4.4 ITERATIVE STATEMENTS

Iterative statements are statements which consist of a **head** and a **body**. The head contains an expression whose value determines whether the body is to be executed initially and/or once again.

4.4.1 *WHILE* STATEMENT

A WHILE statement in C has the form

```
while (expression)
    statement
;
```

In this iterative statement the test which determines whether the loop should be executed or terminated is at the top of the loop. This is similar to a while statement in Pascal. It is executed as follows:

1. The expression following the keyword **while** is evaluated.

2. If the expression evaluates to 0 the loop terminates. Otherwise go to step 3.

3. The statement portion of the loop is executed.

4. Go to step 1.

The body of the loop could be a NULL statement. Here are some examples:

```
/* example1—demonstrates a way of reading a line being typed in */
/* The function getchar returns a character from the standard
        input file, which is often the keyboard.
        The character obtained is stored in ch. As long as the
        character is not a newline character (that is as long as
        Return is not pressed) or the array a is not filled, the
```

character is stored in the array a. The array a does not
contain the newline character.
*/

```
i = 0;
while ( ( (ch = getchar() ) != '\n') && ( i < MAX ) )
    a[i++] = ch;
```

/* example 2–demonstrates an exchange sort */
/* The elements of a are sorted in ascending order
    The array will be sorted if all its elements are arranged in
    ascending order. We will set sorted to 0 to indicate that they
    may not be in the proper order.
    While sorted is 0, ! sorted evaluates to non-zero, we first set
    sorted to 1. We then go through the array and exchange
    adjacent elements if they are out of order. If an exchange
    takes place then we set sorted to 0. This indicates that the
    array has to be examined again.
*/

```
sorted = 0;
while ( ! sorted ) {
    sorted = 1;
    for (i = 0; i < MAX; i++ ) {
      if ( a[i] > a[i+1] ) {
        t = a[i];
        a[i] = a[i + 1];
        a[i + 1] = t;
        sorted = 0;
      }
    }
}
```

4.4.2   *DO-WHILE* STATEMENT

A DO-WHILE statement in C has the form

```
do
    statement
while (expression);
```

In this iterative statement the test which determines whether the loop should be executed or terminated is at the bottom of the loop. This is similar to a repeat-until statement in Pascal. It is executed as follows:

1. The statement(s) following the keyword **do** and up to the keyword **while** is (are) executed.

2. The expression following the keyword **while** is evaluated.

3. If the expression evaluates to a non-zero value then the loop continues. Otherwise go to step 1.

The body of the loop could be a NULL statement. Here are some examples:

/* example1–demonstrates a way of reading a line being typed in */
/* The function getchar gets a character from the standard input
   file which we are assuming is the keyboard. That character is
   stored in a[i] and i is incremented. This continues while
   Return has not been pressed and the incremented value of i
   is less than MAX.
   This is different than the similar example in the preceding
   section. Here the Return or newline character is stored in
   the array. In the example above that character was not
   put into the array.
*/

```
    i = 0;
    do
        ch = getchar();
        a[i++] = ch;
    while ( (ch != '\n') && (i < MAX) );
```

/pagebreak/

/* example 2–demonstrates an exchange sort */
/* The elements of a are sorted in ascending order
   The array will be sorted if all its elements are arranged in
   ascending order. We will set not_sorted to 0 to indicate
   that they may already be sorted.

52

We go through the array and exchange adjacent elements if they are out of order. If an exchange takes place then we set not sorted to 1. This indicates that the array has to be examined again.

```
*/
    do
        not_sorted = 0;
        for (i = 0; i < MAX; i++) {
          if ( a[i] > a[i+1]){
            t = a[i];
            a[i] = a[i + 1];
            a[i + 1] = t;
            not_sorted = 1;
          }
        };
    while ( not_sorted );
```

4.4.3 *FOR* STATEMENT

A FOR statement in C has the form

```
for ( expression1 ; expression2 ; expression3 )
    statement ;
```

It is much more general than the FOR or DO statement in Pascal or FORTRAN, respectively. There is no restriction on the type of expressions used. They may even be NULL expressions, no expressions. Typically **expression1** initializes some variable(s), **expression2** is a test to determine whether the loop should continue or terminate, and **expression3** updates the loop variable(s). If, for example, there is no **expression2** then the only way to exit the loop is from some statement within the body (such as a break, return, or goto).

The FOR statement is executed as follows:

1. expression1 is evaluated and the value discarded.

2. expression2 is evaluated. If it evaluates to 0 then the loop terminates, otherwise go to step 3.

3. The body of the loop is executed.

53

4. expression3 is evaluated and the value is discarded.

5. goto step 2.

The FOR statement is normally terminated when expression2 evaluates to 0. The statements break, goto, and return would allow for premature exit from the loop.

Here are some examples

```
/* example 1 */
/* initialize an array */
    for ( i = 0; i < 10; i++)
        a[i] = 0;


/* example 2 */
/* move to a specific character in an array */
    char a[MAX]; ch*; c;
    •
    •
    •
    for ( ch = a; *ch!= c; ch++ )
        ;


/* example 3 */
/* 'infinite' loop. No exit condition is specified. */
for( avtemp = 0 ; ;avtemp += temp ) {
    scanf( "%g", &temp);
    /* if temp is greater than or equal to MAX_TEMP then we
        exit via the statement goto SHUT_DOWN
    */
        if ( temp >= MAX_TEMP ) {
            printf(" \b\b\b Temperature ALARM!, TEMP = %g \n", temp);
            goto SHUT_DOWN;
        }
    plottmp ( avtemp, temp );
    difftemp = abs(avtemp – temp);
    /* if difftemp is greater than or equal to 10 percent of
        avtemp then we exit via the break statement.
    */
```

```
        if ( difftemp >= 0.1*avtemp ) break;
}
```

4.5   TRANSFER OF FLOW OF CONTROL STATEMENTS

C has a group of statements which allow for transfer of flow of control of execution from one point within a function to another point. They are

BREAK statement   CONTINUE statement
GOTO statement   RETURN statement

4.5.1   *BREAK* STATEMENT

The BREAK statement is used in two situations:

1. To alter the flow of control within a loop or iterative statement, and

2. within a switch statement.

This statement consists of the keyword **break** followed by a semicolon.

When it is used in a loop, control is transferred to the first statement following the loop. Here is an example.

```
i = 0;
do
    rep [i] = num % rad;
    if ( i > 9 ) break;
    i++;
    num /= rad;
while ( num > 0 );
for (j = i; j >= 0; j − −)
    printf( "%d", rep[j]);
```

If i is greater than 9 then we exit the loop and execute the **for**

55

statement.

The statement **break**; is used within a SWITCH statement to transfer control to the statement immediately following the end of the SWITCH statement.

4.5.2   *CONTINUE* STATEMENT

The CONTINUE statement consists of the keyword **continue** followed by a semicolon. This statement is used within loops or iterative statements. Execution of a **continue**; skips all remaining statements in a loop and the loop test is evaluated. Here is an example

```
while ( x < 10 ) {
    tmp = aray[x];
    x++;
    if ( tmp < 0 )
        continue;
/* if tmp < 0 then all following statement until } are ignored */
    sums = sqrt( tmp + 1) + sums
    cnt++;
}
```

4.5.3   *GOTO* STATEMENT

The GOTO statement has the form **goto identifier**;. It transfers control unconditionally to the statement whose label is **identifier**. It may be used to transfer control within a function. Statement labels must be unique within a single function. They cannot conflict with the name of a variable or function. Here is an example of several **goto** statements in two separate functions. The same name may be used for a label in separate functions.

```
fun1(int a, int b, char *p)
{
        .
        .
        goto trap1;
        .
        .
```

56

```
        goto trap2;
            •
            •
    trap1: .....
            •
            •
    trap2: .....
            •
            •
}
fun2 (double x, unsigned int f)
{
            •
            •
        goto trap1;
            •
            •
    trap1: .....
            •
            •

}
```

4.5.4 THE *RETURN* STATEMENT

A RETURN statement is used to terminate execution of a function. It may also be used to return a value. There are two possible forms

    return;

or

    return expression;

In the first case no value is returned by the function. In the second case the value of the expression is returned. The type of the expression is converted to the type of the function. Here are some examples:

```
void example1 (int x, int y, char *z)
{
•
•
return;
```

57

```
    •
    •
}

double example2(float x,float y, int *z)
{
    •
    •
return ( x+y/*z[i]); /* result of expression is converted to double */
    •
}
```

4.6 *NULL* STATEMENT

The NULL statement consists of a semicolon. Some examples of its use are

```
/* While loop with empty body */
    while( *strptr++) ; /* move pointer to end of string */

/* Take no action in some instance of a switch */
switch tok-val of {
    INT_VAL: readint( tok );
        break;
    REA_VAL: readrea( tok );
        break;
    ID:
    FUNC: ;
    default :unxpect( tok );
}
```

CHAPTER 5

DECLARATIONS

Declarations are used to associate identifiers with data objects and to give information about the lifetime of data objects. Variables, constants, types, structures, and functions are declared to the translator or compiler. The compiler may then allocate space for these objects, determine which operations may be applied to these objects, determine any conversions that are necessary, and also determine in which portions of the program the variable will exist. Also, a data object may be assigned a specific storage class.

5.1 USE OF IDENTIFIERS

All identifiers must be declared. A declaration conveys information about the type and lifetime of an identifier. The lifetime or **scope** refers to the portion of a program in which an identifier may be used. Identifiers may always be used in the block in which they are declared. Identifiers that are declared in one function or file may be used in another provided the appropriate **linkage** is established. This allows for several portions of a program to be compiled separately. An identifier may be used for different purposes within a function provided that it is possible to uniquely identify the purpose. This is called the **name space** of an identifier. By default an object has **auto-**

matic storage duration. This means that an object comes into existence each time a function is called and goes out of existence when a function terminates. However, if it is declared to have a **static storage duration**, it exists or retains its value from one activation of a function to another. Identifiers declared within a block have similar lifetimes.

5.1.1 SCOPE OF IDENTIFIERS

An identifier has meaning within a specific region of a C program. The **scope** of an identifier is that region. We discuss the scope of an identifier as it refers to a block, a function, or a file.

An identifier declared at the beginning of a block has a scope that extends until the end of the block. Its scope will extend through every block contained within the first block, unless it is declared anew within a contained block. If it is declared within an inner block then its scope includes the portion of the text after the interior block. In the following example the first identifier named x has a scope consisting of lines $2 - 4$ and $10 - 11$. An inner block has a declaration of x which is a different identifier than the original. The new x has scope from lines $6 - 9$. The variable z has scope consisting only of lines $6 - 9$. We cannot refer to z outside of that scope. The scope of the identifier y is lines $2 - 11$.

```
1:  {
2:      int x, y;
3:          x = 1; y = 1;
4:          x = x + y;
5:      {
6:          int x, z;
7:              z = 1; x = 2;
8:              z: x + y;
9:      }
10:     x := x + y;
11: }
```

The scope of a label consists only of the function in which it is used. Thus a goto may only transfer control within one function. Likewise the scope of the parameters of a function are restricted to that function. In the following the identifiers x, y and label1 have scope restricted to the function fun1.

```
int fun1(double x, char y)
{
    •
    •
label1:
    •
    •
}
```

An identifier declared outside of a block has scope for all following blocks unless the identifier is declared anew within an inner block. Below, the identifier **top** has a scope which goes from its point of declaration to the end of the file, except for the body of the function **fun1**. The scope of the identifier **stack** is the remainder of the file.

```
    •
    •
int top;
float stack[100];
float push (float x)
{
    •
    •
}
char fun1(int x, int y)
{
    float top;
    •
    •
}
float pop
{
    •
```

```
    •
}
```

Unless **top** or **stack** are declared local to a block (as top was with within fun1), they are available or "public" to any function that follows them in the file. They are not available to any function that precedes their declaration in the file. Thus scope may be used to make identifiers public or private within a file.

5.1.2 LINKAGE OF IDENTIFIERS

The scope of parameters to functions or identifiers declared at the head of a block is that function or block. They are known in their scope, may be used there, and have space allocated for them. A C program may consist of several functions that are in separate files or program translation units. The files may be compiled separately. It is possible for identifiers, functions or variable names, to be shared among separate files. It is possible to make some identifiers private to a given file or function. The **linkage** of an identifier refers to whether the identifier is "public" – can be shared by other units, or "private" in the sense that it can only be used in one file.

An identifier may have no linkage, internal linkage, or external linkage. If it has no linkage then it is known only within its own scope and may not be used elsewhere. Examples of this are identifiers that occur in a typedef (they are the name of a type) and the parameters of a function. An identifier declared within a block has no linkage unless its declaration contains the keyword **extern**. An identifier has internal linkage if its scope is limited to one file or program translation unit. The name of a variable or a function may be made internal if the keyword **static** is used. An identifier has external linkage if its scope extends over more than one file.

Here is an example of a program that exists in two files. The files may be compiled separately. The object files are linked by a program called a 'linker'.

```
/* Contents of File 1 */          /* Contents of File 2 */
main(void)                             int x;
{                                 static int zz;
    fun1 ( int );                 fun2(void);
    fun2 (void);                  {
    extern int x;                      •
    int y;                        }
       •
    fun1 (y);
    fun2 ( );
}
int w;
fun1 (int z);
{
    int x;
       •

}
```

In **File 1** the variable **x** in **main** is declared using the keyword **extern**. This means that it is declared in another file and space is allocated for it when that file is compiled. Thus the **x** **in File 2** is made public to **File 1**. The variables y, z, and x in fun1 have no linkage. The variable **w** has internal linkage.

In **File 2** the variable x has external linkage, because File 1 contains a declaration **extern** int x. It is important to remember that it is defined in this file, although it may be declared elsewhere. The variable zz has internal linkage and cannot have external linkage, because the keyword **static** is used. Using **static** makes the identifier private.

5.1.3   NAME SPACE OF IDENTIFIERS

The same identifier may be used for different purposes. For example, the identifier name may be used as a label, the name of a simple identifier, and the name of a field in a struct such as student.name. These uses of the same identifier cause no confusion because the compiler keeps different name spaces. These names spaces are

63

1. objects, functions, typedef names, and enum constants

2. labels

3. tags of structures, unions, and enumerations

4. members of each structure or union individually.

5.1.4   LIFETIMES OF OBJECTS

An object that is declared within a block or function, exists only when the statements in that block are being executed. Each time a block or function is entered a new instance of the object is created (unless we use the key word **static** in its declaration). When the block or function is left the current instance is destroyed or discarded.

5.2   THE FORMAT AND TERMINOLOGY OF DECLARATIONS

The format of a declaration consists of a declaration specifier, followed by a declarator list, followed by a semicolon. For example,

```
static int aray[10], zz, x = 0;
```

Here **static** int is the declaration specifier and the remainder up to the semicolon, is the declarator list. Declaration specifiers may be either storage class specifiers, type specifiers, or type qualifiers. In the example above **static** is a storage class specifier and int is a type specifier.

5.3   STORAGE CLASS SPECIFIERS

The storage for an object is classified as one of two primary classes: **automatic** and **static**. An object has **automatic storage class** if it exists only when the block which contains it is being executed. An object has **static storage class** if its existence is independent of a block of the current program. In addition to these primary classes, an object may be a type definition, it may be stored in a register, or it may have an external storage class which indicates that it is defined elsewhere.

The storage classes available are:

Type of Storage Class	Storage Class Specifier
automatic	auto
register	register
static	static
external	extern
type definition	typedef

If a storage class specifier is not used when a declaration is made then an object in the declarator list is given a default storage class. That storage class depends upon where its declaration appears. If an object is declared within a block or function then its default storage class is auto. Functions declared within functions are taken to be **extern**. If it is declared outside any block then it is assumed to be **static** with external storage class.

5.3.1 AUTOMATIC DECLARATIONS

An object if given storage class auto with a declaration of the form

auto type-specifier declarator-list;

The auto storage class may only be used within functions and blocks. This establishes storage for the object(s). An instance of such an object is created when the function or block is entered and it is discarded when the function or block is left.

5.3.2 REGISTER DECLARATIONS

An object if given storage class register with a declaration of the form

register type-specifier declarator-list;

65

A register declaration is equivalent to an auto declaration. Additionally it implies, that the object will be stored in a register of the computer. This is not necessarily the case and it varies among implementations. However, it is not possible to obtain the address (use the & operator) of an object of register storage class. This means that an object of register storage class cannot be modified by a pointer.

5.3.3 STATIC DECLARATIONS

An object if given storage class **static** with a declaration of the form

static type-specifier declarator-list;

If an object is declared **static** inside a block then the object exists whether the block that contains it is being executed or not. Storage is allocated for it during compilation and the object retains its value throughout the life of the program. If the declarator list contains an initialization, then the object is initialized once. In the following example the object **times_called** is initialized to 0 and retains its value from invocation to invocation of **fun**.

```
double fun (double seed)
{
    static long int times_called = 0;
    times_called++;
    printf("The function 'fun' has been called %l times \n",
                                        times_called);
    •
}
```

If an object is declared **static** outside of a block then the object's lifetime is the same as the program, and it has internal linkage. This means that it may only be referred to in any block following its declaration within the file in which it is declared. Its use is restricted to one file and it is private to that file.

5.3.4   EXTERN DECLARATIONS

The declaration **extern** is often used for objects that are defined in one file and are also to be used in another. An object declared using the **extern** specifier must have a definition somewhere else in one of the files that make up the C program. That means it must be declared either with static storage class in the same file or be declared without **extern** storage class in some other file. Declaring the object by one of these means causes the object to be defined in the sense that space is allocated for it. If it is declared with a **static** storage class in another file then it cannot be declared with **extern** storage class. An object with **extern** in its declaration has external linkage if it is defined in another file. If it is defined in the same file and the storage class is **static** then it has internal linkage. Here is an example.

```
/* Contents of File 1 */          /* Contents of File 2 */
main(void)                             /* definition and declaration of x */
{                                 int x;
/* declaration of x               static int zz;
   external linkage */            fun2 ()
      extern int x;               {
/* declaration of y                   •
   internal linkage                   •
      extern int w;               }
      fun1 ( int );
      fun2 (void);
         •
      fun1 (w);
      fun2 ( );
}
static int w;
fun1 (int z);
{
      int x;
         •
}
```

In **File 1** the variable **x** in **main** is declared using the keyword **extern**. This means that it is declared in another file or later on in the same file. Space is allocated for it when that declaration is compiled. The declaration of **x** in **File 2** is the definition of **x**. The variable **w** in **main** is declared using **extern**. It is declared and defined later on in **File 1**. This is internal linkage.

5.3.5 TYPEDEF DECLARATIONS

The **typedef** specifier is used to associate an identifier with a type. It doesn't create a new type or allocate storage. It does provide a means to give a synonym to an existing type. For example

```
typedef char Alpha[30]; /* here Alpha is an array of
                10 characters */
Alpha wordin, wordout; /* wordin and wordout are type Alpha
                or and array of 10 characters */

/* A new type keyword called Inform is created. An object of
    this type will be a struct as described here. */
typedef struct info {
        Alpha name;
        char ssnum[9];
        int age;
        char gender;
        float salary;
} Inform;

/* A new type keyword called Link is created. An object of this
    type will be a pointer to a struct whose tag is node. */
typedef struct node *Link;

/* A new type keyword called List_element is created. An object
    of this type will be a struct as described here */
typedef struct node {
    Inform worker;
    Link next;
}    List_element;

Alpha names [100];      /* an array of 100 objects of type Alpha */
Link *head, *tail;      /* head and tail are pointers to list elements */
```

68

5.4 TYPE QUALIFIERS

The qualifier **const** is used to specify that an object will never change its value once it has been initialized. Such an object is called a constant. The qualifier **volatile** is used to indicate that an object may change its value without any action of the program. The object may be controlled by hardware or some combination of hardware and software external to the program.

5.4.1 THE CONST QUALIFIER

If the const qualifier is used in a declaration then the declared object may be initialized, but not modified after that. For example, after the declarations

```
const int i = 10;
int *pint;
```

it is not allowable to write **pint = &i;** If that were allowed, it would be impossible to modify **i** by a statement such as *p = 23; also note that **i** was initialized to 10. **const** can be used effectively with function parameters. Consider

```
fun ( const char *s, char *t)
```

Here both **s** and t are pointers to characters. The object **s** may only be used to examine the characters to which it points. They may not be modified and so are protected from changes by the function. The object t may be used to examine and modify the characters to which it points.

5.4.2 THE VOLATILE QUALIFIER

An object may be declared **volatile**. This means its value must be checked every time it is used. This reduces the possibilities for optimization since it is not possible to store the value in a temporary location for use in a sequence of statements. It would be reasonable to declare an object whose value is the system clock as volatile. It would also be reasonable to declare that object as const, since it should not be modified by a program.

5.5 TYPE SPECIFIERS

Type specifiers name the data type of the object being declared. Some name the elementary or simple data types and others name the derived types.

5.5.1 SIMPLE SPECIFIERS

The simple specifiers are those which name the simple data types. They are:

void	char	short
int	long	float
double	signed	unsigned

5.5.2 STRUCTURE SPECIFIERS

An object which is a struct data type may be declared in one of three ways

1.   struct {member-list} identifier -list;

2.   struct structure-tag identifier-list;

3.   struct structure-tag {member-list} identifier-list;

In each of those ways the identifier-list may be empty. Here are examples of each

```
/* example of 1. */
    /* objects named a, b, and p are declared. The first two are
      structures and the third is a pointer to a structure
      described here. Without a tag the structure definition
      can't be used again.
    */
      struct {int x, y; char color;} a, b, *p;
```

```
/* examples of 2. */
    /* objects named a, b, and p are declared. The first two are
       structures and the third is a pointer to a structure whose
       tag is point. That structure must be defined elsewhere.
    */
        struct point a, b, *p;

    /* This is an incomplete declaration. The structure named
       point must be defined elsewhere
    */
    typedef struct point *p;

/* examples of 3. */
    /* The structure tag point is declared here. We may use it
       elsewhere for declarations of objects or in typedef
       constructions.
    */
    struct point { int x,y; char color; };

    /* objects named a, b, and p are declared. The first two are
       structures and the third is a pointer to a structure whose
       tag is point. That structure is defined here.
    */
    struct point { int x,y; char color; } a, b, *p;
```

5.5.3   UNION SPECIFIERS

Union specifiers follow the same rules as structure specifiers. The only difference is that the keyword **union** is used instead of structure.

5.5.4   ENUMERATION SPECIFIERS

Enumeration specifiers follow the same rules as structure specifiers, except for two differences. One is the keyword **enum** is used instead of structure. The other is the elements of the member list have the form

identifier or identifier=constant-expression

Here are two examples:

```
enum colors { red, blue, green } pallete;
enum colors { red = 10, blue = 20, green = 30 } pallete;
```

5.6 DECLARATORS

C provides a greater variety of possibilities for declarators than most languages. In the declaration,

```
static int x, *p, (pfun) (), ax[10], (*pfax[]) ();
```

static and **int** form the declaration specifiers of the declaration and **x, *p, (*pfun) (),** and **ax[10]** form the declarator list. **x** is a simple declarator, ***p** is a pointer declarator, **(pfun) ()** is a function declarator, **ax[10]** is an array declarator, and **(*pfax[]) ()** declares **pfax** to be an array of pointers to functions.

5.6.1 SIMPLE DECLARATORS

Simple declarators are identifiers. If we represent the declaration specifier portion of a declaration by SPEC, then I in the declaration SPEC I is a simple declarator. They are used to declare variables of arithmetic, enumeration, structure, and union types. In these cases the type specifier of a declaration provides all typing information. This is the case in

```
int i; and
struct term { int ser_num, model_num; float time; } t0,t1;.
```

5.6.2 POINTER DECLARATORS

Pointer declarators are used to declare objects of pointer type. If we represent the declaration specifier portion of a declaration by SPEC, then *D in the declaration SPEC *D is a pointer declarator. In this case D would be a pointer to the type given in SPEC. Here are some examples.

```
p is a pointer to an integer –
    int *p;
```

```
pa is an array of pointers to objects of type float –
    float *pa[ ];
```

72

pfun is a function which returns a pointer to char –
    char *pfun( );

pchar is a pointer to char. The value of pointer is constant, it always points to the same location, and is initialized to the address of ch. The variable ch may be modified –
    char ch, *const pchar = &ch;

pchar is a pointer to const char. Although the value of pchar may change, but the object to which it points may not be modified through pchar –
    const char *pchar;

5.6.3   ARRAY DECLARATORS

Array declarators are used to declare objects of array types. If we represent the declaration specifier portion of a declaration by SPEC, then D[constant-expression] in the declaration SPEC D[constant-expression] is an array declarator. In this case D would be an array to the type given in SPEC. Here are some examples.

ar is an array of 10 integers and ard is a two dimensional array with 5 rows and 7 columns –
    int ar[10], ard [5] [7];

pa is an array of pointers to objects of type char –
    char *pa[ ];

pa is a pointer to an array of objects of type char –
    char (*pa) [ ];

5.6.4   FUNCTION DECLARATORS

Function declarators are used to declare objects of function types. If we represent the declaration specifier portion of a declaration by SPEC, then (D) ( ) in the declaration SPEC (D) ( ) is a function declarator. In this case D would be a function to the type given in SPEC. Here are some examples.

funi is a function which returns an integer value and funia is an array of functions returning an integer value –
    int funi( );
    int (funia[ ]) ( );

pfunl is a pointer to a function returning an integer –
    int (*pfuni) ( );

In the examples above, we didn't list any parameters for the functions. We will discuss listing parameters now. There are two styles for declaring parameters in functions. The "old style" is common in versions of C based on the original definition by Kernighan & Ritchie. The "new style" is part of the ANSI standard for C and is available in many C compilers on micro-computers.

OLD STYLE

– parameters declared and listed only when the function is defined

– parameters listed in function definition, and declared on
    following lines

– declaration of a function in another function or block consists of
    name followed by parentheses

NEW STYLE

– parameters declared and listed whenever the function is declared

– parameters listed and declared within parentheses following
    name of function

Here is an example:

OLD STYLE	NEW STYLE

```
OLD STYLE                NEW STYLE

main ( )                 main(void)
{   float a,b,c;         { float a, b, c;
    int d[20];             int d[20];
    double cubrt ( );      double cubrt(float x,float y,float z,int d[ ]);
        •                      •
        •                      •

}                        }
double cubrt(x,y,z,w)    double cubrt(float x, float y, float z, int w[ ]);
float x,y,z;             {
int w[ ];                    •
{                           •
```

74

```
            •                    }
            •
}
```

The declaration of cubrt in **main** in the "new style" is called a prototype. Writing it that way allows a reader to know the types of the arguments to a function. It also may allow for the compiler to check that the types of the arguments to a function are correct.

5.6.5   READING COMBINED DECLARATORS

Declarators may be combined. Here are some examples.

```
int *pa[ ]        pa is an array of pointers to integers
int (*pa) [ ]     pa is a pointer to an array of integers
int (*pa[ ]) ( )  pa is an array of pointers to functions
                  each of which returns a value of type int.
```

How should these be read and understood. The key is to work from the innermost parentheses that enclose the identifier.

1. Put parenthesis around the declarator.

2. Find the identifier.

3. Go right token by token to the enclosing right parenthesis ')', to determine whether the identifier is an array, function, etc.

4. Go back to the enclosing left parenthesis (, and go right to determine if it is pointer, etc.

5. Continue with steps 2 and 3 until all parentheses have been considered.

This is demonstrated below.

Start with int *pa [ ].

   1. We rewrite it as int (*pa [ ]).
   2. We have the identifier pa.
   3. Going right we see it as an array.
   4. Going back to (we see that it is an array of pointers).

Since the type is int we have a declaration of an array of pointers to integers.

75

Start with int (*pa) [ ]

1. We rewrite it as int ((*pa) [ ]).
2. We have the identifier pa.
3. Going right to) gives no more information.
4. Going back to (and then to * we see that pa is a pointer.
2. Going right we see that we have a pointer to an array.

No more information is to be gained within the outermost parentheses so we have that pa is a pointer to an array of integers.

Start with int (*pa[ ]) ( ).

1. We rewrite it as int ((*pa [ ]) ( )).
2. We have the identifier pa.
3. Going right to) we see that pa is an array.
4. Now go back to (and we have that pa is an array of pointers.
2. In the next level of parentheses we see that each element of the array is a function.

So we have declared an array of pointers each of which is a pointer to a function of type int.

5.7 INITIALIZERS

Declarators can be used to initialize an identifier. In this case the identifier is initialized to the given value at the beginning of its lifetime. Some examples are

static int i = 10;   /* i is initialized to 10 */.

int zz = i + 3;   /* zz is initialized to the value of i plus 3 */.

char c[10], *p = c;   /* p is a pointer and initialized to the
                            address of the array c */

Scalar objects are initialized in the manner given in the next two sections. Arrays, structures, and unions require further discussion.

5.7.1 INITIALIZATION OF OBJECTS WITH STATIC STORAGE DURATION

Objects with **static** storage duration, declared with the keyword **static**, are by default initialized to 0. Otherwise they may be initialized in a declaration such as **static int i = 10;**. The value given during the initialization is the initial value of the object during its lifetime. The value given may be a constant or another expression. Here are two examples.

```
static char c; *p = &c;
```
c is initialized to ASCII NULL and p is initialized to the address of c.

```
static int i = 10; j = (i++) *3;
```
i is initialized to 10, j is initialized to 30, and i is incremented.

5.7.2 INITIALIZATION OF OBJECTS WITH AUTOMATIC STORAGE DURATION

Objects with automatic storage duration, declared with the keyword **auto** or no storage class, are not automatically initialized to any value. An equal sign = must follow the declarator, which in turn is followed by a constant or an expression. The value given during the initialization is the initial value of the object during its lifetime. Here are two examples.

```
char c = '\0'; *p = &c;
```
c is initialized to ASCII NULL and p is initialized to the address of c.

```
auto int i = 10; j = (i++) *3;
```
i is initialized to 10, j is initialized to 30, and i is incremented.

5.7.3 INITIALIZING ARRAYS

Array elements may be initialized by providing a list of expressions for the elements. These expressions must consist of constant values. The value for each element, except for the last element, is followed by a comma. The ANSI standard for C allows initialization of auto or **static** arrays. Other C compilers only allow initialization of arrays with **static** storage class. Here are some examples with explanations.

```
int aray[5] = { 1, 2, 3, 4, 5 }
```
The five elements of aray are given the values 1, 2, 3, 4, 5.

```
int aray[ ] = { 1, 2, 3, 4 }
```
When the size of the array is not specified, the number of elements is determined by the initialization. So here we have an array of size 4.

```
float aray[2] [3] = {
    { 1.4, 4.5, 6.7 },
    { 3.4, −233.6, 17.2}
}
```
Here aray is an array of two rows and three columns. The inner curly brackets are optional. We may declare the identical object with
```
float aray[2] [3] = {
    1.4, 4.5, 6.7, 3.4, −233.6, 17.2
}
```
Another way to declare this is with
```
float aray[ ] [3] = {
    { 1.4, 4.5, 6.7 },
    { 3.4, −233.6, 17.2}
}
```
This is because array elements are stored in memory by rows, in row-major order with the rightmost subscript varying the fastest.

Here an array of strings is initialized.
```
char *storclass[ ] = {
    "auto",
    "extern",
    "register",
    "static",
    "typedef"
}
```

Finally, it is not necessary to initialize all elements of an array. Those not specified are initialized to 0. For example,

```
int diag[4] [4] = {
    { 1 },
    { 0, 1 },
    { 0, 0, 1 },
    { 0, 0, 0, 1 }
}
```

initializes an array with 4 rows and 4 columns so that there are 1's on the main diagonal and zeros everywhere else.

5.7.4   INITIALIZING CHARACTER ARRAYS

Arrays of characters may be initialized to a string. For example,

```
char messg[ ] = "Error on line %d\n";
```

initializes the array **messg** to the string. This array includes the ASCII character '\0'. It could be modified later by setting

```
messg[6] = 'a'; messg[7] = 't';
```

A declaration of the form

```
char messg[10] = "Error";
```

sets all elements of messg to '\0' following the final 'r'.

5.7.5   INITIALIZING STRUCTURES

Structures may be initialized in a manner similar to arrays. For example,

```
struct student {
    char name[30];
    char gender;
    float average;
} typical = {
    "Jasmine", 'F', 85.34
}
```

Once the struct is established we may initialize an array of structures such as

```
struct student class [ ]{
    { "Ernest", 'M', 78.89 },
    { "Lynn", 'F', 83.56 },
    { "Karl", 'M', 82.45 },
    { "Marie", 'F', 79.45 },
    { "Oliver", 'M', 90.34 }
}
```

It is not necessary to initialize all elements of a structure. This,

```
struct student typical = {
    "Rochelle"
}
```

initializes the identifier typical to have name field of Rochelle. The other fields are not initialized.

Finally, we may initialize a structure to a value from an outer block with a statement such as **struct student new = typical**;

5.7.6 INITIALIZING UNIONS

The elements of a union may be of different types and any initialization refers to the first item. For example in

```
union inval {
    int intval;
    float fltval;
    char chval;
} tester = 3;
```

the int field will be used and 3 will be assigned to intval.

5.8 TYPE NAMES

Type names are used in several situations: with the sizeof operator, with cast operations, and with function prototypes. The name of a type must be specified without the name of an object. For example (char *)p, casts p as a pointer to a character. Any possible type name may be constructed such as

```
float              /* float */
float *            /* pointer to float */
float [10]         /* array of 10 objects of type float */
float *[10]        /* array of 10 pointers to objects of type float */
float (*)[ ]       /* pointer to an array of an unspecified number
                      of objects of type float */
```

80

float *( )	/* function of unspecified number of parameters returning a pointer to float */
float (*[ ]) (void)	/* array of unspecified size, of pointers to functions with no parameters returning a pointer to object of type float */

CHAPTER 6

FUNCTION AND PROGRAM STRUCTURE

Previous chapters have dealt with specific elements of the language C, but have not addressed the issue of the structure of programs and functions. Here we discuss functions, recursion, issues relating to using the function **main** with parameters (command line arguments), program status, and finally the structure and flow of control of the collection of functions in a program.

The ANSI standard for C is most noticeably different from earlier versions in regards to the declaration of functions. We'll call the ANSI standard version "NEW" and the other "OLD". Examples will be given for both versions where it is appropriate. They will be labeled "OLD" and "NEW".

6.1 FUNCTION DECLARATION AND DEFINITION

A function declaration gives the type of the function and the name of the function. The ANSI standard for C requires that types of the parameters also appear in a declaration. A declaration, then, provides the specifications for calling the function and the type of value returned. The definition of a function consists of the declaration and statements necessary to specify the action taken by the function.

6.1.1 DIFFERENCES BETWEEN ANSI STANDARD AND EARLIER VERSIONS OF C

The ANSI standard version of C is most noticeably different from earlier versions in regard to the declaration of functions. We'll call the ANSI standard version "NEW" and the other "OLD". Here are two examples of definition of a function as it appears in "OLD" and "NEW" styles.

"OLD" Style	"NEW" Style
| ```
double dotprod(x,y,n)
double x[ ], y[ ];
int n;
{
      int i; double temp = 0.0
      for (i = 0; i < n; i++)
            temp = x[i]*y[i] + temp;
      return (temp);
}
``` | ```
double dotprod( double x[ ], y[ ],int n);
{
int i; double temp = 0.0;
      for (i = 0; i < n; i++)
temp = x[i] * y[i] + temp;
      return (temp);
}
``` |

In the "OLD" style the parameters to the function are declared on the line(s) following the function declaration. Also, the types of the parameters were not listed with the names of the parameters in its declaration. The declaration in the "NEW" version requires that the parameters be listed with their type.

If a function or parameter is not declared then it is assumed to be type int. The function **power** above, will return a value of type double and so must be declared wherever a call to the function occurs. In the "OLD" style it was sufficient to declare it without mentioning the parameters as

double power ( );

In the "NEW" style the types of the parameters must be listed

83

as well

```
double power( double [ ], double [ ], int );
```

This notation allows a compiler to check that the arguments in a call to the function are in the correct order, are the correct type, and are the proper number. It also makes it easier for a reader to understand the program.

6.1.2 FUNCTION DECLARATION

A function declaration which accompanies the definition of a function is of the form

"NEW" Style   —   return-type function-name (parameter declarations);

"OLD" Style   —   return-type function-name (parameter list) parameter declarations;

The return-type is the type of the function, the type of the value returned by the function. An example is

"NEW" Style   —   int getline (char *s, int max);

"OLD" Style   —   int getline (s, max)
                        char *s;
                        int max;

If the function is being declared not at its definition, but in the context of a call to the function, then the "NEW" style declaration is no different. In the "OLD" style the declaration is

```
return-type function-name ( );
```

If a function does not contain a return statement, then its return-type is void. The return-type for a function may not be a function or an array. The valid return types for a function are:

arithmetic types   structure   union   pointer   void.

A function may only be declared with storage class extern or static. If no storage is given then it is assumed to be extern.

The parameters of the function may not have any storage class declaration except for register, may not be initialized, and are assumed to be of type int unless a type is declared. If a function has no parameters then it may be declared as

    return-type function-name (void)
or
    return-type function-name ( )

6.1.3 PROTOTYPES

A **prototype** is a declaration of a function which contains information regarding the types of the parameters, but need not contain names for the parameters. This is used in the "NEW" style when a function is declared separate from its definition. For example, if the function from the previous section, **getline**, were to be called from **main** then **main** would have to contain a declaration of the form

    int getline (char *, int);

The purpose of the prototype is to provide information to the compiler so that the type, number, and order of parameters may be checked during translation. This checking was not present in some "OLD" style versions of C, so prototypes were a convenience for the reader, if they were available at all.

6.1.4 FUNCTION DEFINITION

A function definition consists of a declaration and the collection of statements that determine what a function does. The definition is the block of a function. The following is a definition of a function which returns the dotproduct of the two vectors or arrays x and y. We assume that each array has n elements. Line 1 is a declaration and the remainder is the block.

```
1:   double dotprod( double x[ ], y[ ], int n);
2:   {
3:       int i;   double temp = 0.0;
```

85

```
4:        for (i=0;  i<n; I++)
5:            temp = x[i] *y[i] + temp;
6:        return (temp);
7:  }
```

The parameters of the function have the function as their scope, may not have any storage class declaration except for register, may not be initialized, and are assumed to be of type int unless a type is declared.

The remainder of the function definition consists of the block or body of the function. As it is a block, it begins with { and ends with }. The contents of the block are declarations and statements. Functions may not contain the definition of another function; they may not be nested and are all on the same level. Naturally, a function may call another function. If a function is to return a value then it must contain a return statement. The value returned by a function is the value of the expression in the return statement. Execution of an instance of a function terminates when a return statement is executed or when the flow of control leaves no more statements before the final } to be executed.

Consider the following:

```
1:  int bsearch ( Int item, int list [ ], in n)
2:  {
3:      int low = 0, high = n – 1, mid;
4:      while ( low <= high ) {
5:        mid = (low + high)/2;
6:        if ( item < list[mid] )
7:           high = mid – 1;
8:        else if ( item > list[mid] )
9:           low = mid + 1;
10:       else
11:          return mid;
12:     }
13:     return –1;
14: }
```

This function performs a binary search for **Item** within the array **list**. If **item** is in **list** then the function returns its position. Otherwise, it returns −1. Line 1 contains the declaration. The parameters are **item, list,** and **n**. Lines 2 − 14 are the block or body of the function. If we ever get to statement 11 then the function terminates and returns the value **mid**. Otherwise, we assume that statement 13 will eventually be executed and the function will return a value of −1.

6.1.5 VARIABLE ARGUMENT LISTS

Most functions are written with a fixed number of arguments, but it is possible to define functions that take a variable number of arguments. **printf** is an example of such a function. In that case, not only may the number be variable, but also each type of the arguments may be variable.

The definition and calling of functions with a variable number of arguments may differ between "OLD" style compilers and those that meet the ANSI Standard. Here we discuss methods compatible with the ANSI Standard. In order to define a function with a variable number of arguments:

1. The header file <stdarg.h> must be included in the source file that contains a function with a variable number of arguments. This defines a type va_list, a macro va_arg, and a function va_end for use with variable argument lists.

2. The function must be declared with ellipses (...) following the fixed parameter list, e.g., int summer (int count, ...).

3. The number of arguments used when calling the function must be equal to or greater than the number of fixed parameters, e.g., in our example summer(count) is valid as is summer(count, num1, num2, num3).

4. The header file <stdarg.h> must be included in the source file that contains a function with a variable number of arguments. This defines a type va_list, a macro va_arg, and a function va_end for use with variable arguments lists.

5. A variable of type va_list must be declared in the function.

6. va_start must be applied to the variable immediately preceding the ,... in the function declaration.

7. va_arg is used to get items of the proper type from the argument list.

8. va_end must be called before a return is executed.

Here is an example which produces the output

```
    sum = 1
    sam = 6
    sum = 3
#include <stdio.h>
#include <stdarg.h>                          /* 1. inclusion of header file */
main (void)
{   /* 2. declaration of summer indicates variable argument list */
    int summer ( int count, ...);
    int num1 = 1, num2 = 2, num3 = 3, sum = 0;
    sum = summer (1, num1);                  /* 3. call to summer */
    printf( "sum = %d\n", sum);
    sum = summer (3, num1, num2, num3);      /* 3. call to summer */
    printf( "sum = %d\n", sum);
    sum = summer (2, num1, num2);            /* 3. call to summer */
    printf( "sum = %d\n", sum);
}
/* 2. declaration of summer indicates variable argument list */
int summer (int count, ...)
{
  /* 4. The variable ap is declared of type va_list */
    va_list ap;
    int n, sum = 0;
  /* 5. va_start is applied to count. Access to the arguments
     following count is provided this way. */
    va_start(ap, count);
    for(n = 1; n <= count; n++)
        sum = sum + va_arg(ap, int);         /*6. va_arg retrieves
                                               an item type int */
```

88

```
    va_end(ap);                    /* 7. clean up before return */
    return sum;
}
```

6.2   FUNCTION ARGUMENTS AND PARAMETERS

The identifiers appearing in the identifier list of a function declaration are referred to as the formal parameters or parameters of a function. The identifiers appearing in the identifier list of a call to a function are referred to as the actual parameters or arguments of a function. In the following statements, for example, **x,y,** and **z** are names of parameters and **name1, scores,** and **ave** are arguments.

```
/* declaration */
/* three parameters
    x – array of char,              y – array of int,
    z – pointer to a function returning double with one parameter
*/
char *mark ( char x[ ], int y[ ], double (*z) ( int y [ ] ) )
/* call to function mark */
pch = mark (name1, scores, ave);
```

The number of arguments must be the same as the number of parameters in the declaration, unless a variable number of arguments is indicated in the declaration. In the latter case the number of arguments must exceed or match the number of parameters listed in the declaration.

The arguments may be evaluated in any order. This means that it is possible that one compiler translates the statements

```
i = 12;
access(i ++, a[i] );
```

as **access (12, a[13])**, while another compiler may translate them as **access(12,a[12])**. The element of **a** whose value is passed to **access** is determined by the order of evaluation. It is not a good idea to write programs whose results depend upon the order of evaluation of arguments to a function.

All arguments are passed by value. This means that the argument is evaluated and its value is made available to a function to take the place of the parameters. This also means that a function cannot modify any of its arguments, only the value of its arguments. To have a function modify an object, it must receive the address of the object. If the address of an object is an argument then the function cannot modify the address but it may modify the contents of the address. For example a function which would swap the contents of two integer objects would be written as

```
void swap( int *x, int *y)
{
    int t;
    t = *x;
    *x = *y;
    *y = t;
}
```

Here is an example of a call to the function.

```
int house1, house2;
swap(&house1, &house2);
```

The & operator is used to make the addresses available to the function. Arrays and functions used as arguments don't need the & before their names. Arrays and functions evaluate as addresses in a function call. Thus elements of arrays may be modified through functions. Here is an example of a function that copies one string to another. The first implementation uses arrays and the second pointers. The functions achieve the same results and either may be called with arguments that are arrays or pointers to char.

```
void strcpy( char s[ ], char t[ ])
{
    int i = 0;
    while ( (s[i] = t[i]) != '\0')
```

```
        i++;
    }

    void strcpy( char *s, char *t)
    {
        while ( (*s = *t) != '\0') {
            s++;
            t++;
        }
    }
```

6.2.1 ARGUMENT CONVERSION RULES

The types of the arguments to a function are converted to the types of the parameters in the declaration. It is best to have a prototype declaration wherever the function will be called. In that case the conversions are performed as if by assignment. For example,

```
float fun1 ( float x); /* prototype declaration */
char *fun2 ( char *pc); /* prototype declaration */
    •
    •
fun1(12);        /* 12 converted to 12.0 float real */
fun2(0);         /* 0 converted null character pointer */
```

If no prototype is present then the automatic conversions take effect. In the previous example, without a prototype the 12 in the call to fun1 would be converted to double instead of float.

6.2.2 PASSING DERIVED TYPES

Arrays of a specific type are passed as pointer to that type. The following prototypes are thus equivalent.

```
int ( char aray[ ] )
int ( char *aray )
```

If a function is a parameter then the corresponding argument is passed as a pointer to a function. If we have the prototype

```
void msort ( int a1[ ], int a2[ ], int (*cmp) (int n, int m) )
```

and the call to the function

```
msort (aray1, aray2, numcomp )
```

then the address of numcomp is passed to msort so that the function numcomp may be called from msort.

6.3   RETURN VALUES

A function returns a value to the point at which it is called. If the function doesn't contain a return statement then the function must be type void. If a function is any other type then execution of the function must terminate with a return statement. The expression in the return statement is evaluated, converted to the type of the function, and then transmitted to the calling statement.

6.4   EXECUTION OF FUNCTIONS

When a function is called the arguments are evaluated and those values are copied into the objects represented by the parameters. All local variables, those contained within the beginning {, are created each time a function is called, unless they have storage class static. Execution then continues statement by statement until

1. A return statement is executed. Control then returns to the caller.

2. The function finished execution of statements in the function block. Control then returns to the caller.

3. The function calls another function. When the called function terminates, control usually returns to the point at which it was called and execution continues.

4. An error occurs or some other signal occurs which aborts execution.

6.5 RECURSION

A function may call itself directly or indirectly through another function. This is termed **recursion** and is allowed in C. When a function is called recursively new copies of the parameters and automatic local variables are created. They are separate from any previous invocation of the function. When the current invocation of the function terminates, control is passed to the point of call and the newly created parameters and local variables are discarded. Here is an example which contains a function **nfac(int n).** That function computes the factorial of a recursively. The example also demonstrates that a static variable, **j** in this case, retains its value from one call to another of the function in which it is declared. It also shows that an automatic variable, **i** in this case, starts anew each time the function in which it is declared is called.

```
#include <stdio.h>
#define MAX 6
main (void)
{
    int nfac (int n);
    int n = MAX;
    printf(" In main, n = %d, n factorial = %d\n", n, nfac(n) );
    n = 0;
    printf(" In main, n = %d, n factorial = %d\n", n, nfac(n) );
}

int nfac(int n )
{
    int i = 10; static j = 10;
    if ( n < 0 )
        return 0;
    else if ( n == 0 || n == 1 )
        return 1;
    else {
        i = i + 1; j = j + 1;
        printf (" TESTING automatic i = %d, static j = %d,
            parameter n = %d\n",i,j,n);
```

93

```
        return (n *nfac (n − 1) );
    }
}
```

The output is

```
TESTING automatic i = 11, static j = 11, parameter n = 6
TESTING automatic i = 11, static j = 12, parameter n = 5
TESTING automatic i = 11, static j = 13, parameter n = 4
TESTING automatic i = 11, static j = 14, parameter n = 3
TESTING automatic i = 11, static j = 15, parameter n = 2
In main, n = 6, n factorial = 720
In main, n = 0, n factorial = 1
```

6.6 PROGRAM PARAMETERS–COMMAND LINE ARGUMENTS

Every C program has one function whose name is **main**. It is the first function executed of the functions in a program. If **main** is declared as

"OLD" Style	or	"NEW" style

```
"OLD" Style         or        "NEW" style

main ( )                      int    main(void)
{                             {
    •                             •
    •                             •
}                             }
```

then the program has no arguments. If we were in a UNIX environment and the program were named prog, then it would be invoked by typing prog and pressing return. If we were in a MS-DOS environment and the program were named prog.exe, then it would be invoked by typing prog and pressing return. The function **main** is declared with no arguments so it is invoked by entering only its name. It is possible to allow for arguments to be entered when the program is invoked, for arguments to be part of the command line. In that case **main** is declared as

```
"OLD" style                 or        "NEW" style
main (argc, argv)                      int   main (int argc, char *argv[ ] )
int argc;                              {
char *argv[ ];                         •
{                                      •
    •                                  }
    •
}
```

When the program begins execution, two arguments are passed
to **main**. The first argument, traditionally named **argc**, has as
its value the number of arguments on the command line includ-
ing the name of the program. The second argument, traditionally named **argv**, is an array of pointers to char or an array of
strings. The array **argv** holds the name of the program and any
arguments that are part of the command line. Blanks are used
to delimit or separate the arguments. The first string, **argv[0]**,
is the program name, and the other arguments are stored in
argv[1] through **argv[argc−1]**. **argv[argc]** is a null character
pointer. Here are some examples.

```
add table1 table 2    −    argc = 3    argv[0] = add
                                        argv[1] = table1
                                        argv[2] = table2

sort −n −u +f myfile   −    argc = 5    argv[0] = sort
                                        argv[1] = −n
                                        argv[2] = −u
                                        argv[3] = +f
                                        argv[4] = myfile

sort                  −    argc = 1    argv[0] = sort
```

Here is an example of a program that copies one file to another.
Both files must be specified on the command line so that argc
must be three. It doesn't do too much except demonstrate the
use of argc and argv.

95

```c
main ( int argc, char *argv[ ] )
{
    FILE *fromfile, *tofile;
    int c;
    if (argc != 3) {
        printf(" %s: Incorrect number of arguments\n", argv[0]);
        printf(" Correct usage: %s file1 file2\n", argv[0] );
    }
    else {
        if ( (fromfile = fopen( argv[1],"r") ) = = NULL ) {
            /* couldn't open file to read from.
                print error message and return status 1 */
            printf("%s: couldn't open %s for reading\n",
                    argv[0], argv[1]);
            return 1;
        }
        else
        {
        if ( (tofile = fopen( argv[2], "w") ) = = NULL ) {
            /* couldn't open file to write to.
                print error message and return status 2 */
            printf("%s: couldn't open %s for writing\n",
                    argv[0], argv[2]);
            return 2;
        }
        else {
            /* all is well */
            while ( ( c = getc(fromfile) ) != EOF )
                putc ( c, tofile);
            /* return status 0 */
            return 0;
        }
    }
}
```

6.7 PROGRAM STATUS

The function **main** is type int. It returns a value, to the operating environment, called the program status. It may be used to signal normal termination of a program or an error situation. In the example in the preceding section the program status was used as

status 0   all complete with no known problems
status 1   couldn't open source file for reading
status 2   couldn't open destination file for writing

6.8   FLOW OF CONTROL

Program execution begins with the function **main**. After that point control is handled as in any other function. Control is passed back to the operating system when **main** terminates or some other function causes execution to terminate.

CHAPTER 7

THE PREPROCESSOR

The C preprocessor is software that processes directives before the source program is translated. The directives are part of the source file(s). Almost every directive begins with the character #. They allow files to be included as part of the source program, allow for conditional compilation of portions of the source program, and allow for text and macro substitution. The preprocessor may be used to construct programs that are easier to develop, easier to read, and portable in the sense that they may be transferred from one machine to another. The following is a list of the directives that will be discussed in this chapter.

define	elif	else	endif	error	if
ifdef	ifndef	include	line	pragma	undef

The directives may be placed anywhere in a C program. When they are used they are preceded by a # and possibly some white space. For example, both **#define** and **# define** are valid in ANSI Standard C. In previous versions of C, directives had to be written with the # in column one and no white space. Preprocessor directives are assumed to end at the end of the line. If a preprocessor directive or any C code is to extend over a line then the backslash character, \, may be used to "splice" lines. We mean that

```
        a = 123 \
    .246
and
        #define MAX \
            23
```

are equivalent to

```
        a = 123.246
and
        #define MAX 23
```

This "line splicing" is done before the program is split into tokens.

7.1 TRANSLATION PHASES

A program is compiled or translated in several phases. Errors may occur at any phase and cause the translator to not go on. The phases are

1. Trigraph sequences are replaced by their equivalents.

2. Whenever a backslash \ precedes a new-line, the two physical lines are "spliced" to one logical line.

3. The source text is split into tokens and white space. Comments are replaced by a single space.

4. Preprocessing directives are followed. This may cause going through phases 1– 4 recursively.

5. Escape characters and string literals are replaced by their equivalents.

6. Adjacent string literals are concatenated.

7. All tokens are analyzed and translated both syntactically and semantically. This is known as the parsing phase.

8. The output of the previous phase is translated to machine code or some intermediate code. If necessary optimization may be

performed during this phase. This is the end of compilation.

9. External data and function references are resolved during the link phase. Library functions and objects are obtained and joined with the rest to form a module which may be executed.

7.2 MACRO DEFINITION AND EXPANSION

7.2.1 THE #DEFINE DIRECTIVE

The **#define** directive allows for the association of meaningful identifiers with constants, keywords, statements, or expressions. It has one of two forms:

```
#define identifier token-sequence
```
or
```
#define identifier( identifier-list ) token sequence
```

The first is called a **manifest** and the second a **macro**. If an identifier has been defined then it may not be re-defined differently in the same source program, unless it is "erased" by use of the **#undef** directive. It may be defined to the same value more than once in a source file. The token-sequence doesn't end in a semicolon and must be on one "logical" line. It could span more than one "physical" line if the line splice character \ is used.

First we will discuss manifests. Every occurrence of the identifier, following the manifest in the source file, is replaced with the token sequence. This occurs before the program is complied. Substitutions are only made for tokens and are not made within quoted strings. For example, the definition **#define DONE 0** defines the name **DONE**. There will be no substitution for **DONE** in **NOTDONE** or in **printf("DONE")**. Here is a program that contains some manifests.

```
#define IF          if
#define ENDIF       ;}
#define THEN        {
#define ELSE        ;} else {
```

```
#define MAX            23
#define MIN        (-(MAX + 1) )
#define STRINGS         char*
#include <stdio.h>
main(void)
{
    int index[MAX], a = MIN;
    STRINGS p;
#define ERRMESS1          " Could not create index. \
Failed due to insufficient information.\n"
    IF ( MAX < -MIN )
    THEN
      printf(ERRMESS1)
    ELSE
      printf("Please continue\n")
    ENDIF
```

The preprocessor changes it to

```
- -the file stdio.h is placed here
main(void)
{
    int index[23], a = -24;
    char *p;
    if ( 23 < -(-24) )
    {
      printf(" Could not create index. Failed due to
        insufficient information.\n")
    ;} else {
      printf("Please continue\n")
    ;}
}
```

Now we discuss **macros**. A **macro** may be thought of as being similar to a function. Both have parameters and both may be accessed in a program by writing the name of the macro/function followed by a list of arguments within parenthesis. The difference is that a function call is translated to an evaluation of arguments followed by a jump instruction, whereas a **macro** expands to in-line code. For example,

```
#define MIN(A,B)            ((A) < (B) ? (A) : (B))
```

defines a **macro** named MIN. If it is used in the body of a program as

```
z = MIN( x+z, x*z);
```

then the preprocessor replaces it with

```
z = ( (x+z) < (x*z) ? (x + z) : (x*z) );
```

The definition gives the replacement text for the **macro**. As for manifests, substitutions are made only for tokens and no substitutions are made within quoted strings.

Some care has to be taken when using and writing macros. The **macro** MIN above has side effects with a statement such as MIN(x++, y++);. The smaller of the two gets incremented twice. Parentheses should be used when writing a **macro** to insure proper evaluation. For example,

```
#define AREA(L,W)  L*W
```

used as

```
z = AREA( x+z, x*z );
```

would be replaced with

```
z = x+z * x*z
```

which is not what was intended. A better definition would be

```
#define AREA(L,W)   ( (L) * (W) )
```

Using a macro instead of a function will reduce execution time of a program. It eliminates the time required to call and return from a function. The standard header file, stdio.h, often contains macro definitions for getchar and putchar. This reduces the time to handle characters.

No substitution is made within quoted strings. However, an argument can be expanded into a quoted string by the use of # in front of the parameter. For example,

```
#define wherex(stmnt)          printf(#stmnt " executed\n")
```

when used as

```
wherex(x = a+b;);
```

will be translated as

```
printf ("x = a+b;"" executed\n");
```

The strings are concatenated and we end up with

```
printf("x = a+b; executed\n");
```

When ## is in a macro, the two tokens on either side of the ## are concatenated into one token. For example, if we define

```
#define REVERSE(X,Y) Y ## X
```

then REVERSE("abc","def") produces "def""abc". Adjacent strings are concatenated so we end up with "defabc".

7.2.2   THE #UNDEF DIRECTIVE

Once a name has been defined through the use of **#define**, it cannot be redefined to a new value within a file unless **#undef** is used. For example, suppose MAX has been defined as **#define** MAX 10. To change its value or make it undefined later in a file, use **#undef** MAX.

7.3   FILE INCLUSION

A preprocessor directive of the form **#include** <filnam> causes the replacement of that line by the contents of the file filnam. It is also valid to use **#include** "filnam". The two forms indicate the search path to be taken for finding filnam. When the file name is enclosed in < >, some implementation dependent path is searched for the file. This usually means that the locations of the necessary header files is searched first. When the file name is enclosed in " ", the current directory is searched first for the file. **filnam** may also include a path as part of the file name. Here are some examples

#include <stdio.h>	This will include the file stdio.h from the system dependent directories
#include "stdio.h"	This will search the current directory for stdio.h
#include <sys>types.h>	Here the file name has a patch associated with it
#include "menu.def"	The local directory is searched for a file named menu.def
#define FILENAME file 1 #include "FILENAME"	The file name comes from another pre-processor directive

Nesting is allowed in files that are included using **#include**. That means if file1 is

```
#include <stdio.h>
#include <ctype.h>
#include "menu.def"
```

then the line **#include** "file1" is processed as if the include directives from file1 were present.

7.4   CONDITIONAL COMPILATION

Directives are available to cause lines of the source file to be ignored or selectively sent to the preprocessor or compiler. Conditions may be checked to determine whether to skip a section of the source code. This is often to make C programs portable, easy to transfer from one machine to another. The directives used are

    #if   #elif   #else   #endif

The **#if** and **#elif** are used with a constant expression; sizeof, type casts, and enumeration constants are not allowed. They may use the preprocessor operator defined. Its syntax is defined(identifier). If the expression evaluates to a non-zero value then it is taken to be true. If it evaluates to 0 then it is taken to be false. Naturally, **#if** must have a matching **#endif**; **#elif** and **#else** cannot be used without a preceding **#if**, and the directives **#elif** and **#else** go with the most recent **#if** or **#elif**. Some examples follow.

```
#if WRDSIZ > 16
    #define SHFT 32
    #define REGTYPE long int
    #define LONGWRD       1
#else
    #define SHFT      16
    #define REGTYPE int
#endif
    •
    •
REGTYPE x,y;
#if defined(LONGWORD)
    void lngshft( REGTYPE, int);
#endif
    •
    •
#if defined(LONGWRD)
    lngshft(x,SHFT-n);
#endif
    •
    •
#if defined(LONGWRD)
    void lngshft( REGTYPE a, int b)
    {
        •
        •
    }
```

If **WRDSIZ** is greater than 16 then the next three **#define** directives are presented to the preprocessor. Otherwise the two following the **#else** are seen by the preprocessor. The next statement declares **x** and **y**. If LONGWORD has been defined,

105

the declaration for the function lngshft, the call to lngshft, and the definition of lngshft are presented to the compiler. Otherwise, the compiler never sees them!

```
#if TTY = = RTYPE
    #include "rterm.h"
#elif defined (PLOTTER)
    #include "plot.h"
    #if PLOTTER > 2
        #include "colorp.h"
    #endif
#elif PRINTER = = LASER
    #include "pscript.h"
#elif defined (PRINTER)
    #include "prntr.h"
#endif
```

This example selects header files to be included. Note that the directive **#elif PRINTER = = LASER** does not apply to the directive **#if PLOTTER > 2** because of the preceding **#endif**.

7.5   OTHER DIRECTIVES

The #line directive has two possible forms.

#line constant

or

#line constant "FILENAME"

The compiler internally stores the current line number and file name. Using a preprocessor directive such as #line 23, changes the internally stored line number to 23. Using a preprocessor directive such as #line 234 "module1.c", changes the internally stored line number to 234 and the file name to module1.c.

The preprocessor directive #error used as #error token-sequence causes the preprocessor to write a diagnostic message that includes the token sequence.

The preprocessor directive #pragma token-string causes the

preprocessor to perform an implementation-dependent action. For example, in Microsoft C 5.1 optimizing compiler, the pragma loop_opt is available to control optimization for loops. Using #pragma loop_opt(on) turns on loop optimization for loops that follow and #pragma loop_opt(off) turns it off.

The two directives **#ifdef** and **#ifndef** perform the same task as the **#if** used with defined(identifier). However, they are not a part of the ANSI Standard. They are available in some compilers to be compatible with previous versions of C.

7.6   PREDEFINED NAMES

The ANSI Standard contains several identifiers that are pre-defined and can be used to produce special information. They may not be redefined or undefined. They are

LINE

A decimal constant containing the current source line number.

FILE

A string literal containing the name of the file being com-piled.

DATE

A string literal containing the date of compilation, in the form "Mmm dd yyyy"

TIME

A string literal containing the time of compilation, in the form "hh:mm:ss"

STDC

The constant 1. This will be defined only in implementa-tions that meet the ANSI Standard.

CHAPTER 8

THE STANDARD LIBRARY

Early versions of C had no standard library of functions and no standard collection of header files. However, a large number of support functions were and are in common use. While they are not standardized, the same functions appear in almost every implementation of C. The number and type of the parameters and even the names of the functions vary, unless the version of C conforms to the ANSI Standard definition of C.

Each library function has an associated header file that must be included to use the function. There are well over 100 library functions required by the Standard. Some implementations provide many more which are often application or hardware dependent. An example would be collection of library routines for graphics on an EGA monitor on a MS-DOS system.

A selection of the library functions in the ANSI Standard will be listed or discussed below. There are too many to list them all. Consult documentation available with your C compiler for a complete list. The functions are grouped according to the standard header files, as each must have the appropriate header file included before its use.

8.1 INPUT/OUTPUT <stdio.h>

<stdio.h> contains prototypes, types, and macros that account for almost one third of the library. There are functions for

file operations – such as
    int fclose(FILE *filnam)
    FILE *fopen(const char *filnam, const char *mode)
    int remove(const char *filnam)
    int rename(const char *oldnam, const char *newnam)

character input and output –
  get or put a character or a string to a file
    int fgetc(FILE *filnam)
    char *fgets (char *s, int n, FILE *filnam)
    int fputc(int ch, FILE *filnam)
    int getc(FILE *filnam)
    int putc(int ch, FILE *filnam)
    int ungetc(int ch, FILE *filnam)

  get or put a character or string to standard input or output
    int getchar(void)
    char *gets(char *s)
    int putchar(int ch)
    int puts(const char *s)

  direct input and output functions –
    size_t fread(void *p, size_t size, size_t numobj, FILE *filnam)
    size_t fwrite(const void *p, size_t size, size_t numobj, FILE
        *filnam)

  file positioning functions – such as
    int fseek(FILE *stream, long offset, int origin)
    void rewind(FILE *filnam)

  error functions –

```
void clearerr(FILE *filnam)
int feof(FILE *filnam)
int ferror(FILE *filnam)
void perror(const char *s)
```

formatted input –

We discuss the functions **fscanf** and **scanf**. **fscanf** is used for formatted input from a file different from the standard input file. **scanf** is equivalent to **fscanf(stdin,...)**. Their prototypes are

```
fscanf(FILE *stream, const char *format, ...)
```
and
```
scanf( const char *format, ...)
```

stream is a pointer to an object of type **FILE**. **FILE** is declared in stdio.h. Format is a string which contains conversions specifications, which describe the form of the input. Names of identifiers go in place of ..., and each of those must be a pointer. The functions return the number of input items fetched, converted, and assigned, and returns EOF (defined in stdio.h) if the end of file is reached.

The format string may contain

1. Whitespace characters to match whitespace in input.

2. Ordinary characters, except for whitespace and %. If such a character is in the format string, the next character of input must match that character. If not, **scanf** returns.

3. A conversion specification for the next input field. The data is interpreted appropriately and assigned to the next argument in the identifier list. A conversion specification begins with a % followed by an optional * which means that the assignment is suppressed, an optional number indicating the width of the input field, an optional h, 1 or L indicating the width of the object to which the values will be assigned, and a required conversion character. The conversion characters are given in the table below. Using * reads the data but doesn't assign it to the object to

110

which the next identifier points. The number of columns in the input field is specified by width. If an h precedes a conversion character of d, i, n, o, or u then the argument is a pointer to short rather than int. If an I precedes a conversion character of d, i, n, o, or u then the argument is a pointer to long rather than int. If an I precedes the conversion characters e, f, or g then the argument is interpreted as a pointer to double rather than float. If an L precedes the conversion characters e, f, or g then the argument is interpreted as a pointer to long double rather than float.

For example, **scanf("$ %4d.%2d", &dol, &cent)** reads a $, a blank, the next four columns and assigns them to dol., a ., and the next two columns and assigns them to cent. **fscanf(fil, "%6f,%s,%3hd", &ave., name, &Idno)** reads six columns into ave. as type float, a string of non-white space characters to *name, and a 3 column decimal integer into idno which has been declared as short.

CONVERSION CHARACTERS FOR scanf, fscanf

Character	Input Data Form	Data Type of Argument
d	decimal integer	int *
i	integer – octal if leading 0, hexadecimal, if leading 0x	int * int *
o	octal integer w/wo leading 0	int *
x	hexadecimal integer w/wo leading 0x	int *
u	unsigned decimal integer	unsigned int *
c	character. The next input characters (width tells how many) are put into the listed array. This is not a string, no \0 is added.	char *

111

s	string of non-white space characters, not quoted. Width gives the length of the string. Terminating \0 is added.	char *
e,f,g	floating point number. The input format is an optional sign, a string of numbers possibly containing a decimal point, and an optional exponent field containing an E or e possibly followed by a signed integer.	float *
p	pointer value	void *
n	the number of characters read so far, doesn't increase the number of characters read	int *
[...]	matches the longest non-empty string of input characters from the set between brackets, a \0 is added.	char *
[^...]	matches the longest non-empty string of input characters not from the set between brackets, a \0 is added.	char *

For example, scanf("%[0123456789]" strptr); will gather input stopping when it finds a character that is not a digit, and scanf("%[^0123]",strptr); will gather characters as long as they are not a 0,1,2, or 3.

formatted output –

We discuss the functions **fprintf** and **printf**. **fprintf** is used for formatted output to a file different than the standard output file. **printf** is equivalent to **printf(stdout,...)**. Their prototypes are

    fprintf(FILE * stream, const char *format, ...)
and

```
printf( const char *format, ...)
```

stream is a pointer to an object of type **FILE. FILE** is declared in stdio.h. **format** is a string which contains conversions specifications, which describe the form of the output. Names of identifiers go in place of ... . The functions return the number of characters written or a negative value if an error occurs.

The format string may contain ordinary characters and conversions specifications. The ordinary characters are passed to the output unchanged. The conversion specifications begin with the character % and end with a conversion character. Between the % and the conversion character there may be any of

1. Flags or modifiers
    -   prints left justified in the field
    +   prints a number with a sign always
    0   fills any leading blanks with 0, numeric output
    #   alternate forms of output: for octal the first digit will be 0, for hexadecimal the first characters will be 0x, for float-point output a decimal point will always be included.

2. The minimum field width. If the output is less than the number of columns specified, t will be printed right justified with leading blanks, unless a modifier above had been used.

3. A period which separates field width from precision.

4. A number indicating the precision, the number of characters to be printed to the right of a decimal point in numeric output.

5. A length modifier
    h   —   print as short or unsigned short
    l   —   print as long or unsigned long
    L   —   long double

CONVERSION CHARACTERS FOR printf, fprintf

Character	Input Data Form	Data Type of Argument
d, i	signed decimal notation	int
o	unsigned octal notation, without a leading zero	int
x, X	unsigned hexadecimal notation, without a leading 0x or 0X, using all lower case output for x and all uppercase for X	int
u	unsigned decimal notation	int
c	single character after conversion to unsigned character	int
s	characters from the string are printed until a '//0' is reached or until the width specifier has been satisfied	char *
f	decimal notation of the form mmm.ddd or –mmm.ddd; the number of d's is specified by the precision; the default precision is 6, a precision of 0 suppresses the decimal point	double
e, E	decimal notation of the form m.ddddde+xx, –m.ddddde+xx, m.ddddde–xx, –m.ddddde+xx, or the same forms with E in the place of e; the number of d's is specified by the precision; the default	double

	precision is 6, a precision of 0 suppresses the decimal point	
g, G	general format; %e or %E is used if the exponent is less than −4 or greater than or equal to the precision; %f used otherwise; trailing zeros and the trailing decimal point are not printed	double
p	implementation dependent representation of a pointer value	void *
n	the number of characters written so far by this function call is written <u>into</u> the argument	int *
%	no argument converted, prints %	

Several examples of **printf** occur throughout this text.

8.2 MATHEMATICAL FUNCTIONS <math.h>

A variety of over twenty hyperbolic, logarithmic, trigonometric and utility mathematical functions are available. A few are

```
double sinh(double x)
double cosh(double x)
double ln(double x)
double cos(double x)
double atan(double x)
double sqrt(double x)
```

8.3 CHARACTER CLASS TESTS <ctype.h>

These functions are all type int with one parameter of type int. Some test a character to determine its attributes by returning non-zero if true, 0 if not.

isalnum(int c)	– c is upper/lower case letter or decimal digit
isalpha(int c)	– c is upper/lower case letter
iscntrl(int c)	– c is a control character
isdigit(int c)	– c is a decimal digit
isgraph(int c)	– c is a printing character except space
islower(int c)	– c is a lower case character
isprint(int c)	– c is a printing character including space
ispunct(int c)	– c is a printing character except letter, digit, or space
isspace(int c)	– c is a space, formfeed, newline, carriage return, or tab
isupper(int c)	– c is an upper case letter
isxdigit(int c)	– c is a hexadecimal digit

Two other functions return their argument converted to lower or upper case if the value of the argument is a letter. Otherwise the argument is returned unchanged.

    int tolower(int c)   int toupper(int c)

8.4 STRING FUNCTIONS <string.h>

There are two types of functions in **string.h.** One group manipulates strings; their names begin with **str,** and the other manipulates character arrays; their names begin with **mem.** Here is a sampling.

```
char *strcpy( char *s, const char *t) –
    copy t to s including '\0' returns s

char *strncpy( char *s, const char *t, size_t n) –
    copy at most n characters of t to s, returns s;
    if t has fewer than n characters then pad s with '\0'
```

int strcmp(const char *s, const char *t) –
    compares string s to t, return a value <0 if s<t, 0 if s = = t,
    and a value >0 if s > t

char *strstr(const char *s, const char *t) –
    return pointer to the first occurrence of t in s, or NULL
    if t is not present

void *memcpy(void *s, const void *t, size_t n) –
    copy n characters from t to s, returns s

void *memset(void *s, int c, size_t n) –
    place c in the first n characters of s, returns s

8.5   UTILITY FUNCTIONS <stdlib.h>

This is the "catch-all" or "kitchen sink" of the header files. It contains over 20 functions for a variety of tasks: number conversion, storage allocation, and others. Here is a sample list.

int atoi (const char *s) –
    converts s to int

void *calloc (size_t numobj, size_t size) –
    returns a pointer to space for an array of numobj objects,
    each of the requested size; returns NULL if the request
    cannot be satisfied

int system(const char *s) –
    the string s is passed to the environment for execution

int rand(void) –
    returns a psuedo-random number in range 0 to RAND_MAX

8.6   DIAGNOSTICS <assert.h>

The assert macro is used for diagnostic tests in programs. Its specification is

void assert(int expression)

If **expression** is zero then a message is displayed on the

117

standard error device containing the name of the source file and the current line number and the program aborts.

8.7 VARIABLE ARGUMENT LISTS <stdarg.h>

This contains a collection of macros and functions for writing functions with a variable number of arguments in a portable manner. These are discussed in chapter 7.

8.8 NON-LOCAL JUMPS <setjmp.h>

This contains a macro and a function which allow for jumps from one location to any other within the program. This circumvents the normal call and return sequence for functions. It is useful when control needs to be transferred from out of some deeply nested structure. Its contents are

setjmp – saves state information for use by longjmp
longjmp – restores the state saved by setjmp

8.9 SIGNALS <signal.h>

This header file provides means for handling exceptional conditions that may occur during execution. Exceptional conditions include abnormal termination, zero divide or overflow, invalid memory access, interrupts, etc.

8.10 DATE AND TIME FUNCTIONS <time.h>

Functions and types for manipulating date and time are declared here. Some deal with the amount of time spent on a process and others deal with calendar time, such as date, day, year, hour, minute, and second. For example

clock(void) –
   returns the number of seconds of processor time used by
   the program since beginning of execution

time(time_t *tp) –
   returns the calendar time into *tp if tp is not NULL

8.11 IMPLEMENTATION-DEFINED LIMITS <limits.h> AND <float.h>

These header files contain a collection of constants for the sizes of integral and floating-point arithmetic.

8.12 LOCATION-SPECIFIC INFORMATION <locale.h>

The ANSI standard allows for implementations that contain locale-specific conventions. This allows for C to be an international language. For example things such as decimal point characters and currency characters are defined here.